Gardeners'
World magazine

101 Ideas for a
Wildlife-friendly Garden

1 3 5 7 9 10 8 6 4 2

Published in 2009 by BBC Books,
an imprint of Ebury Publishing
A Random House Group Company

The Random House Group Limited Reg. No. 954009

Addresses for companies within the Random House Group can be
found at www.randomhouse.co.uk

A CIP catalogue record for this book is available from the British Library.

ISBN 9781846077302

The Random House Group Limited supports The Forest Stewardship
Council (FSC), the leading international forest certification organization.
All our titles that are printed on Greenpeace approved FSC certified
paper carry the FSC logo. Our paper procurement policy can be found
at www.rbooks.co.uk/environment

Commissioning editor: Lorna Russell
Project editor: Helena Caldon
Designer: Kathryn Gammon
Picture researcher: Janet Johnson
Production controller: Phil Spencer

Colour origination by: Dot Gradations Ltd
Printed and bound in Germany by Firmengruppe APPL,
aprinta druck, Wemding

**Gardeners'
World** magazine

101 Ideas for a
Wildlife-friendly Garden

PROJECTS AND TIPS TO BRING LIFE TO YOUR GARDEN

Author
Michael Lavelle

BOOKS

Contents

Introduction

Most, if not all, gardeners share a love of wildlife, yet concern that some of these creatures will damage our plants often means people distrust these wild visitors. Few of the creatures you see in the garden, however, will ever cause harm to your plants or bother you in any other way. Indeed, many are actually very useful to have around and do a lot more good than harm. Giving them a helping hand is not only great fun, but can involve the whole family and adds another dimension to your outdoor space.

To give you some inspiration as to how you can encourage wildlife into your garden, this book includes 101 ideas from *Gardeners' World Magazine* that will help make your plot paradise for them. It's organised into six sections, where you can get planting ideas, learn how to create habitats, see how to feed or provide shelter for wildlife, and discover how to make water wildlife-friendly. So have a good read or just flip through the pages and have a go at anything that grabs your interest or suits your garden space.

Whether you are an enthusiastic 'first-timer' in the wildlife garden or a more experienced hand, these ideas are sure to help you get nature back into the garden.

Michael Lavelle
Gardeners' World Magazine

Home to roost

You will need:
- Bird box
- Hammer
- Nails

A bird box is a simple and satisfying way to help garden birds. By providing them with nest sites you help birds raise their young, and they will in turn reward you through their tireless efforts to hunt and eat your garden pests during the coming spring and summer.

Cavity nesting birds such as blue tits need boxes with a small entry hole – 28mm (1⅛in) across. These should be hung in early to mid-January, 2–3m (6–10ft) above the ground. Position them where they are sheltered from the wind and shaded from hot sun (avoid a south-facing site), as strong sun may cause the chicks to overheat. Make sure the birds also have a clear flight path into the box.

Inspect the box in late summer or early autumn and remove any nesting material or other debris, as this can harbour parasites. Add a little clean straw to make it an attractive roost, then, in late winter, clear the box out again ready for the nesting season.

TIP

If birds peck at the entrance hole, it doesn't mean the hole is too small – they are just testing to check it will make a secure home.

Window of opportunity

You will need:
■ Bird box
■ Hammer
■ Nails
■ Some live food
(optional)

Not all birds are attracted to boxes with a hole for an entrance. Robins, wagtails and flycatchers need a box with a front panel that covers only two-thirds of the gap, leaving an open 'window'.

If you decide to use a nest box to help robins, it needs to be placed in a secluded location, such as among the branches of a dense climber or shrub, and protected from prevailing cold winds or hot sun. Remember that robins are highly territorial and will fight, even to the death, if crowded together.

Despite their normally sociable demeanour, female robins generally prefer a good deal of privacy when nesting. They are very sensitive to disturbance during egg laying and incubation, and will desert the nest if they think it has been discovered. So, even in the case of quite tame birds, avoid the temptation to peer into the box to see if it is in use and steer clear of the area at nesting time. If you do visit, look for egg-shell fragments below the nest site, which is a sign that the chicks have hatched.

TIP
Provide some live food, such as mealworms, daily to help both the chicks and the hardworking parents.

High-rise living

You will need:
- Artificial martin box
- Hammer
- Nails

Swallows and house martins are very useful summer migrants, consuming huge numbers of flying insects that they hunt and catch on the wing. House martins in particular can have difficulty finding suitable nest sites in towns and cities, as the smooth walls of modern buildings, or vibration caused by heavy vehicles, often causes their mud nests to fall down – sometimes with nestlings inside.

The answer is to put up an artificial martin box, made of a wood and cement mix, that is attached to an artificial overhang. These can be bought from garden centres or online and then hung just below the gutter line of a house in late winter, ideally between 3–6m (10–20ft) above the ground. Check that the birds will have a clear flight path. Martins need a radius of about 12m (40ft) of unobstructed flying space around the house. These boxes can be painted to match the building and can be easily removed for cleaning.

House martins are very sociable and will more readily use nests that are arranged in groups of two or four, and in time you may manage to attract a substantial colony of these birds. Be patient. House martins will use this type of nest box, but only if they find it.

TIP
If bird droppings are becoming a problem on, say, a patio or path, fix a shelf 25cm (10in) wide about 2m (6ft) below the nest to catch them.

Great balls of fluff

You will need:
- Thin branch or twig, around 30cm (12in) long
- Garden twine
- Various nesting materials

Providing smaller birds like robins, sparrows and tits with a ready-made supply of nesting materials gives them a head start. You can do this using mostly recycled materials.

Select a range of materials such as dry grass, straw, downy feathers or fluffy seed heads, then tease them out and mix them well. Avoid any brightly coloured materials or synthetic (non-compostable) items. Find a thin, forked twig branch around 30cm (12in) long. Gather some of the nesting material together and place it in the forked part of the twig. Wind the twine around it, gradually adding more layers until you have formed the 'ball' shape. Attach some string to the other end of the twig and hang it in the tree.

Nesting materials can be supplied from late winter until well into the summer, and the ball should be hung in clear view between nesting areas and feeders. This not only helps the birds locate the ball, but also means that you'll be able to see which birds are using it.

TIP
Materials from your home can be recycled as nesting materials, such as wool, down from old pillows, string, hair from combs and brushes, shed hair from cats and dogs, cotton threads, or small, thin strips of cloth.

Dusting off

You will need:
- Large shallow pot, saucer, or similar
- Sandy soil or fine sand

Birds can often be seen scratching and loosening patches of dry soil to have a dust bath. This act is very important for feather maintenance – the dust soaks up excess moisture and oil, helps to remove parasites, and may even help them cool down on hot days.

If you have a sandy soil, you can simply leave an exposed patch in a sunny location and loosen the surface a little bit. Always choose a place that is well away from bushes or other features that might hide predators such as cats.

On heavy soils, you might need to make an artificial dust bath. Just take a large shallow pot or saucer, pierce a couple of holes in the base to allow water to drain away, then fill it up with fine sand or sandy soil. Place it in an open, sunny spot and make sure any water that accumulates after rain is drained off.

TIP
Replace the soil in a dust bath periodically, as birds leave droppings and parasites that can build up if not removed.

Go batty

You will need:
■ Bat box made
from untreated
wood
■ Screwdriver
and self-tapping
screw

Traditionally feared and often misunderstood, bats actually rank among the most useful and fascinating garden visitors. Their numbers did decline in the last century, though, through loss of habitat – particularly roosting sites, where they slumber away the daylight hours.

Bat boxes can help provide temporary summer roosts for these night-flying predators. Excellent designs are readily available, usually from the same specialist suppliers that make bird boxes. They are much the same style, except that bats prefer to enter their boxes from underneath, rather than through a visible hole at the front.

When fitting a box, secure it firmly in a sheltered position, as high up as possible – ideally 2m (6ft) above the ground, on a tree or wall. Make sure the entrance to it is clear.

Bat boxes fixed to trees should be placed in threes on all but the sunniest side, as bats change roosting preferences throughout the year. Remember that once your bat box has been put up, you must not disturb it, as bats and bat roosts are protected by law.

TIP
Alternatively, when attaching the box to a tree you can avoid damaging the trunk by using a strap pulled tight around it rather than screws.

Holey appropriate

You will need:
- Short length of untreated timber
- Some old, dry, hollow plant stems or bamboo canes
- Wood saw
- Secateurs
- Some 2.5cm (1in) nails and hammer
- Drill and wood drill bit
- Screwdriver and self-tapping screw

Solitary bees emerge in spring, and after mating the female prepares a nest in a hole or crevice. She then stocks this with nectar and pollen for her offspring. Making a nest site for these bees is very simple – all you need are a few canes or old, hollow, herbaceous stems.

If you are using bamboo canes, choose ones that are approximately 7–9mm (⅓in) across and cut them into equal lengths, about 15cm (6in) long, avoiding knots in the cane. You can also use short lengths of branch with holes of various diameters drilled into it. Push these inside a wooden box made from untreated timber, fixed together at the corners with 2.5cm (1in) nails, gradually filling in all the gaps.

Hang the box in a sheltered, sunny spot, such as under the eaves of a garden shed. Ideally place it at around eye-level and at a slight downwards angle, so water doesn't get into the entrance holes and the developing larvae remain dry.

TIP
Don't glue the canes in place inside the box, as the fumes may be toxic.

Bumbling around

You will need:
■ Flowerpot 20cm
(8in) or more in
diameter
■ Tube or pipe
18mm (¾in) or
more in diameter
and around 30cm
(12in) long
■ Piece of slate
or tile
■ Small amount
of chicken wire
■ Generous
'handful' of
nesting material

Bumblebees are a familiar sight in spring and summer, living up to their name by 'bumbling around' almost ceaselessly in search of nectar to feed their young. Round and quite furry, these friendly garden characters are very different to honey bees, and are often active on cool, dull days.

You can encourage them to stay in your garden by making them a nest box. Start by digging a shallow hole a third to half the depth of the sides of a clay pot (one that is about 20cm/8in or more in diameter). Then fill a cup-shaped wire mesh cradle with dry grass or straw and place it inside the pot.

Fit an entry tunnel made using a wide-gauge hose or pipe, 18mm (¾in) or more in diameter and around 30cm (12in) long. Drill it with a number of small holes, to ensure that any water can drain away quickly. Bend the pipe into a shallow U-shape with one end emerging in the nest ball inside the pot, the other outside. Bury the pot and all but the end of the hose upside down in the hole, and place a slate or tile on top to cover the pot's drainage holes.

TIP
Prepare the bees' nest box in late winter, in good time to accommodate the queens as they emerge from their winter slumber.

Hedge your bets

- Wooden wine (or similar) crate, complete with lid
- Plank of 15cm x 2cm (6in x ¾in) untreated timber – about 120cm (4ft) long
- 25mm (1in) galvanised nails
- Jigsaw, drill and hammer
- 25mm (1in) drill bit

Hedgehogs need a nice dry place in which to sleep through the day, and especially in the winter months when hibernating. Providing them with a sturdy wooden house should entice them to stay in your garden to feast on your garden pests.

Use an existing crate, adding a doorway, entrance tunnel and lid. Cut a hole for the entrance tunnel at the bottom of one side of the crate. Use a drill and a jigsaw and make it around 11cm tall by 15cm wide (4in x 6in). Saw the plank of 15cm x 2cm (6in x ¾in) untreated timber into four 30cm (12in) lengths and nail them together lengthways to make the entrance tunnel. Attach this to the crate by nailing it from the inside.

Drill some holes in the back of the crate for ventilation. Put the box in a quiet corner of the garden, fill it with dry leaves and replace the lid.

TIP
Place the house in undergrowth, hidden among soil and leaves, and ensure the entrance doesn't face north or north-east in order to keep it draught free.

Toad of toad hide

You will need:
■ Old clay pot, about 20cm (8in) in diameter
■ Drill, narrow drill bit and hammer
■ Some loam/sand mixed with leafy compost and moss

Toads feed on a range of insects and invertebrates and are particularly fond of slugs. Indeed, the majority of a toad's diet consists of garden pests, and in a single growing season they'll consume thousands of these. Toads hunt at night, spending the day in cool, dark places, such as this easy-to-make toad hide.

You can make an upturned-pot shelter using an old clay pot that's about 20cm (8in) in diameter. Create a semi-circular entrance, 7.5cm wide by 4cm high (3in x 1½in), on one side of the rim by drilling some holes in the shape of the opening, then gently knocking it out with a hammer.

An even simpler method is to use an old, broken pot laid on its side, so there is a narrow entrance. Place your toad hide in a shady spot, ideally among some covering vegetation and near a source of water.

TIP
Line the floor of the shelter with some loam/sand mixed with leafy compost and moss.

Buckets of beetles

Stag beetles are large and impressive creatures. The males have impressive, antler-like mouthparts, hence their name. The females lay eggs underground, usually near rotting wood, and the larvae live in the wood for up to five years before pupating to become adults. Making a habitat for these endangered beetles is very easy.

Using a craft knife, make holes in the sides and base of a bucket. The holes should be 3cm (1¼in) across, with about 5cm (2in) between each. Choose an area of your garden that will not be disturbed and bury the bucket so the rim is just below soil level. Place a few large stones in the bottom of the bucket, then fill it with bark chippings and a little garden soil. Top it up with fresh bark chippings periodically.

TIP
Even if you are not lucky enough to have these magnificent beetles in your garden, you will find that many other creatures will benefit from this bucket home.

Delicate dwelling

You will need:
- Lacewing box
- Screwdriver and self-tapping screw
- Some fresh straw

Lacewings get their name from the delicate, transparent, pale green wings of the adults. However, it is the tiny 'alligator-like' larvae that consume large numbers of insect pests, making them particularly welcome in the garden.

Adult lacewings hibernate in winter and a lacewing house provides suitable conditions for this. In most winters it can remain outside, but it can also be taken into a cool dry shed during cold snaps, returning it to the garden by early March. In mid-June the straw should be removed and replaced with fresh material.

Place the lacewing house away from trees and buildings. Choose a warm, sunny, sheltered spot, facing away from prevailing winds, ideally on the top of a wooden post or fence, and close to vegetation.

TIP
Put the house outside by the end of August. It's also a good idea to buy and add an attractant chemical to help the hibernating adult lacewings find the house.

Butterfly basket

You will need:
- Large wire hanging basket
- Conifer sprigs
- Moss
- Circle of polythene, the same diameter as the basket
- Potting compost, water-retaining gel and slow-release fertiliser
- Various butterfly-attracting plants (see tip, right)
- Hanging bracket
- Screwdriver and self-tapping screw

If space is especially limited, you can always increase the number of plants you grow by using wall troughs, window boxes and hanging baskets. Placing these on walls and fences will give you a 'third dimension' to your outdoor space. A well-chosen selection of plants in a hanging basket provides a colourful feature that will also attract butterflies and moths.

Line a large wire basket with sprigs of green conifer foliage, packing any gaps with moss raked from the lawn. This re-uses garden waste and provides plenty of crevices for insects to hide in. Line this with a circle of polythene cut from an old compost bag and fill the basket to around two-thirds of its depth with compost, incorporating some slow-release fertiliser and water-retaining gel.

Plant a range of butterfly-attracting species in the basket, putting upright specimens in the middle surrounded by trailing types. Fill any remaining gaps with more compost and water it only once it has been hung up.

TIP
Good butterfly-attracting plants include petunias, trailing lobelias, white alyssum (*Lobularia maritima*), Million Bells (*Calibrachoa* spp.), bur marigold (*Bidens ferulifolia*), *Verbena* x *hybrida*, zonal pelargoniums and twinspur (*Diascia barberae*).

Hanging out

You will need:

- Short length of untreated timber
- Some old, dry, hollow plant stems or bamboo canes
- Section of old hollow log; with its bark
- Handful of straw
- Wood saw
- Secateurs
- 2.5cm (1in) nails and hammer
- Drill and wood drill bit (a range between 3–8mm)
- Screwdriver and brackets

If you want to help a range of useful garden insects, this hanging insect home will attract ladybirds, lacewings and solitary bees. You can make one from pieces of wood such as oak and bamboo – all of which should be untreated.

You also need a section of hollow log, with the bark still attached and some dry straw placed in it. Make an A-shaped roof out of untreated timber and attach it to the log section. Place a piece of log with holes drilled into it at the base, then push the canes in tightly above it, using a hammer to tap them in. Make sure they are a snug fit. Never use glue anywhere, as it can release fumes that may poison the insects.

Hang the finished house from a tree, arch or pergola, in a warm, sunny, sheltered place that is out of prevailing winds.

TIP
Make sure you hang the home close to some vegetation to lure insects in by giving them a nearby feeding site.

Stacks of wildlife

You will need:

- ■ Enough bricks to make a base
- ■ 2 or more wooden pallets
- ■ Thin twiggy branches
- ■ Straw
- ■ Bamboo canes
- ■ Logs
- ■ Drill and drill bits (a range between 3–8mm)
- ■ Roofing felt
- ■ Ridge roof tiles
- ■ Pine cones

Many animals naturally share one habitat, and this stack caters for all, creating a 'block of flats' for garden wildlife. It looks fantastic but also acts as a shelter and home for various species during the warmer months, and especially during the winter when many animals survive by hibernating.

The idea is to provide as wide a range of shelter types as possible, from damp cracks for toads and newts to cosy, dry straw that will suit insects or even small rodents. The aim is not to target any one creature, but to provide a multitude of possibilities.

There are no real rules regarding what to include or what to make it from, but if you can get them, wooden pallets are excellent for providing structure and stability. Be sure to include bricks, twiggy branches, straw or dry grass, and sawn logs drilled with holes, and remember that a stack should be decorative as well as functional. Once you have the basic structure, your imagination can run riot.

TIP
Keep the stack dry by giving it a roof. Place a length of roofing felt under a layer of old, recycled ridge roof tiles.

Holly (*Ilex aquifolium*)

Flowering time:
Spring, followed
by berries from
late summer
onwards

When to plant:
Late winter to
spring

Height:
25m (80ft)

Spread:
8m (25ft)

Hardiness:
Completely hardy

A familiar sight in many gardens, holly is an evergreen plant that forms either a tall shrub or a small tree. It is covered in prickly dark green leaves, and many colourful variegated varieties are also available. Both can be used as either specimen plants or for hedging.

Holly provides nesting cover for birds, which also feed on the berries. It is a food plant for holly blue butterfly caterpillars, and the small, nectar-rich flowers attract bees. The berries are mildly poisonous, though, so this, combined with the prickly leaves, means that it may not be suitable for areas where young children will be playing.

Tolerant of most garden soils in full sun or shade, it is easy to maintain, needing only a dressing of fertiliser in the spring, prior to applying a layer of organic mulch. Holly can be clipped annually in August to maintain a neat and compact shape, keeping it a suitable size for smaller gardens.

TIP
Common holly needs separate male and female plants near to each other for the females to be able to produce the familiar red berries. However, the cultivar 'J.C. van Tol' is self-fertile, so will yield berries if only one plant is grown.

June berry (*Amelanchier lamarckii*)

Flowering time:
Spring, followed
by fruit in summer
When to plant:
Late autumn to
late winter
Height:
10m (30ft)
Spread:
12m (40ft)
Hardiness:
Completely hardy

June berry is a shrub or small tree. The white flowers that appear in spring are followed by round, juicy, dark fruits in autumn. These, combined with the dazzling orange of the autumn foliage, give it year-round appeal.

In spring, pollinating insects are drawn to the flowers – especially solitary bees and butterflies. In summer, the fruits are eaten by birds, particularly starlings, garden warblers, thrushes, chaffinches and greenfinches, as well as mammals such as squirrels and foxes.

It likes fertile, well-drained but moist, acid soils, preferably in full sun or partial shade.
If properly sited this plant is amazingly easy to grow. It flowers very freely and makes a good free-standing specimen, as well as being at home in larger shrub or mixed borders. Choose a multi-stemmed plant to provide more impact in smaller gardens than those with a single trunk.

TIP
The related *Amelanchier laevis* can be a good substitute, being more spreading and shrubby, while still prolific in flower and with autumn colour.

Oregon grape (*Mahonia aquifolium*)

Flowering time:
Spring, followed by berries from late summer

When to plant:
Late autumn to early spring

Height:
1m (3ft)

Spread:
1.5m (5ft)

Hardiness:
Completely hardy

Oregon grape forms a pretty, evergreen shrub with glossy green leaves turning red-purple during the winter. The tight clusters of fragrant, bell-shaped, golden flowers that emerge in late winter and early spring are followed by blue-black berries in late summer.

The flowers are a welcome source of early nectar for bees, but birds, particularly house sparrows and blue tits, also attack the flowers seeking nectar and pollen. The blue-black berries are eaten by mistle thrushes and blackbirds.

This plant is easy to maintain, being tolerant of most soil types (provided it is moist but well drained). It needs little if any pruning and is happiest planted in partial shade and sheltered from strong winds.

Unlike taller species of *Mahonia*, Oregon grape spreads, forming dense ground cover, so it needs space. There are several varieties available, but all are ideally suited to a woodland edge or dappled shade within a shrub border.

TIP
Grow it alongside drifts of daffodils – the flower colours complement each other well.

Daphne (*Daphne mezereum*)

Flowering time:
Late winter and early spring
When to plant:
Autumn to early spring
Height:
1.2m (4ft)
Spread:
1m (3ft)
Hardiness:
Completely hardy

Hidden away for much of the year, this daphne produces fragrant, pink to light purple, sweet-smelling flowers in late winter and early spring, making it an outstanding garden plant.

Daphne's flowers provide early pollen and nectar for insects, especially bees, although birds such as blackcaps have also been known to drink the nectar from the flowers. The red fruits are eaten by finches, thrushes, starlings, tits and warblers.

It thrives in moist, well-drained, humus-rich soil, in sun or partial shade. Once established, it is slow growing and relatively maintenance free. It is best planted among evergreens, which act as a background foil for the flowers. The plant is poisonous, however, and can be a skin irritant when handled, so it may not be suitable for areas where young children will be playing.

TIP
For prolonged interest, underplant it with winter- and spring-flowering bulbs, such as snowdrops and dwarf daffodils.

Crab apples (*Malus* spp.)

Flowering time:
Spring, followed
by fruit from late
summer onwards
When to plant:
Late autumn to
late winter
Height:
Variable, up to 6m
(20ft) or more
Spread:
7m (22ft) or more
Hardiness:
Completely hardy

There are many types of crab apple, all of which share the trait of abundant spring blossom clothing their branches. The fruit that follows often provides a welcome source of food for wildlife.

Crab apple trees support a huge range of wildlife, including crevice-dwelling insects and the caterpillars of more than 20 moth species (such as the eyed hawk moth). The flowers support bees and other pollinators, while the fruits are eaten by birds, rodents and various other invertebrates.

With so many types of crab apple to choose from, you will always find one to suit your garden, although all need good drainage and a sunny but sheltered position to prosper. When grown as a freestanding tree they are relatively easy to maintain.

TIP
If you are short of space, try the Ballerina variety 'Maypole', which is a small, columnar tree. It produces masses of carmine-coloured blossom in early May, followed by large purple fruit in late summer.

Cherries (*Prunus* spp.)

Flowering time:
Spring, followed by fruit from late summer onwards

When to plant:
Late autumn to late winter

Height:
Up to 20m (70ft)

Spread:
Up to 10m (35ft)

Hardiness:
Completely hardy

Cherries are one of the delights of spring, as their flowers appear in spectacular profusion on every branch and twig.

The blossom is a good nectar source for a range of insects, especially bees. Unless protected, the fruits are rapidly devoured by numerous bird species that strip them from the trees almost as soon as they are ripe. Green pug moth caterpillars will eat the leaves.

Cherries thrive in most fertile soils, although they will not do well on acidic ground. They are easy to maintain and fit in well among naturalistic or mixed planting. Being very shallow rooted, they can be problematic if planted as specimens in grass, as the roots often lie on or near the soil surface and can become an obstacle to mowing.

TIP

Wild cherry trees can grow to huge sizes, so choose a small cultivar. 'Celeste' is naturally compact with tasty red fruits and good in pots; *Prunus cerasus* is a small, wild, shrubby species with sour-tasting fruit loved by birds.

Pears (*Pyrus* spp.)

Flowering time:
Spring, followed
by fruit from late
summer onwards

When to plant:
Late autumn to
late winter

Height:
Up to 15m (50ft)

Spread:
Up to 10m (35ft)

Hardiness:
Completely hardy

Pears are at their prettiest in early spring, when the conspicuous, white, star-shaped flowers appear in abundance. In autumn, the leaves turn from dark green to orange and red and act as a perfect foil for the fruit. The trees often prove too large for smaller gardens, however, unless a specifically dwarf variety is chosen. Good varieties include 'Terrace Pearl', which is self-fertile and can be grown in a container or open ground, or 'Garden Pearl', which is also self-fertile.

The flowers are an excellent source of nectar, especially for bees in the spring. Chinese character and eyed hawk moths feed on the leaves, while a profusion of species eat the overripe fruit in autumn.

Any sunny spot on fertile, moist, but well-drained ground will suit a pear tree. The strong vertical branching habit means it will require very little pruning and makes it an excellent choice for a lawn specimen.

TIP
If you're not after edible fruit, try the willow-leaved pear, *Pyrus salicifolia*, which has a profusion of blossom and a gentle semi-weeping habit.

Elder (*Sambucus* spp.)

Flowering time:
Early summer,
followed by fruit
in late summer
When to plant:
Late autumn to
early spring
Height:
6m (20ft)
Spread:
6m (20ft)
Hardiness:
Completely hardy

The elder is a familiar, fast-growing shrub or small tree. It produces abundant cream, musk-scented flowers on flat-topped umbels in summer, followed by round, shiny, black fruits.

A wonderful plant for wildlife, it attracts many species of insects, including bees, flies and hoverflies, and therefore encourages insect-eating birds. The berries are eaten by small mammals and birds, particularly finches, thrushes, starlings and garden warblers.

It is a very tolerant plant, although it is most at home in rich, moist soil, and ideally suited to large shrub borders or a wild garden. Don't prune it every year, though, as it will not flower and so will be of limited use to wildlife.

TIP
If children have access to your garden, plant the native elder *Sambucus nigra*. This species is not poisonous, but some other, related ones are.

Flowering currants (*Ribes* spp.)

Flowering time:
Spring
When to plant:
Late autumn to
late winter
Height:
2m (6ft)
Spread:
2m (6ft)
Hardiness:
Completely hardy

The flowering currant is an excellent dual-purpose plant for the garden, being both highly ornamental as well as great for wildlife. It looks best in spring when the red or rose-pink, tubular flowers are borne in hanging clusters. These are followed by small, edible, if rather unpalatable, berries in summer.

All currants are excellent shrubs for wildlife, providing dense nesting cover for birds if left unpruned. The flowers are popular with bees and bumblebees that visit for nectar, which are in turn hunted by sparrows and tits.

This plant grows well in most moisture-retentive but well-drained soils, and is an extremely useful addition to a shrub or mixed border. The cultivar 'Brocklebankii' adds to the effect with its golden foliage, while 'Tydemans White' has bright white flowers.

TIP
If your flowering currant does not fruit well, try a buffalo currant, *Ribes odoratum*, instead. This reliably bears dark fruits that are eaten by songbirds and small mammals.

Butterfly bush (*Buddleja davidii* 'Peakeep')

Flowering time:
Summer to autumn

When to plant:
Late autumn to
early spring

Height:
3m (10ft)

Spread:
5m (15ft)

Hardiness:
Completely hardy

Buddleia is a large, fast-growing shrub, often known as the butterfly bush as it attracts clouds of butterflies to its nectar-rich flowers. It grows best in a fertile, well-drained soil in full sun.

Many species of butterfly sip nectar from the buddleia flowers, including peacocks, red admirals, commas and small tortoiseshells. Several species of bees also visit it. The seeds are eaten in the winter by birds and small mammals.

Buddleia is a great addition to any mixed or shrub border and as it is available in many cultivars in a range of shades, it easily fits into a colour-themed border. When choosing colours, though, remember that the pink- and lilac-flowered forms attract butterflies more readily than those with dark purple and, in particular, white flowers.

Prune bushes hard back to their woody base every February to keep them to a manageable size and to encourage strong new flowering stems.

TIP
If space is limited in your garden, deadhead this plant so that it can't self-seed.

Hebes (*Hebe* spp.)

Flowering time:
Summer to autumn

When to plant:
Autumn and
spring

Height:
Up to 2.5m (8ft),
depending on
the species

Spread:
Up to 2.5m (8ft),
depending on
the species

Hardiness:
Generally quite
hardy

Hebes are an important group of plants as they include so many highly ornamental species. The flowers range through white or pink to pale blue or lilac and are borne throughout the summer above the somewhat exotic-looking evergreen foliage.

All hebes are popular with bees and several species of butterfly – particularly small tortoiseshells and red admirals – who visit the flowers looking for nectar. Larger specimens also provide dense cover for small creatures so they can hide from predators.

Hebes are easy to grow, with most of them preferring a sunny, sheltered position on any well-drained, neutral to alkaline soil. They are an excellent choice for shrub or mixed borders and the larger species lend themselves well to use as hedging plants in coastal locations.

TIP
Hebes tend to be short lived
and become untidy as they
age, so they are best replaced
every few years.

Lavenders (*Lavandula* spp.)

Flowering time:
Summer
When to plant:
Autumn and
spring
Height:
1m (3ft)
Spread:
1.2m (4ft)
Hardiness:
Most species
are hardy

Lavenders are as important to wildlife as they are to us as gardeners. All of these shrubs are small and aromatic with grey-green leaves. They produce small, nectar-rich, purple, pink or white flowers from mid-summer to autumn.

Great clouds of white butterflies are often seen in large patches of lavender in late summer. They are looking for nectar, but will have to share this with several species of bee that compete for the sugary drink.

Lavenders are best grown in a dry, sunny spot where they develop their fragrant qualities to best effect. They can be used to make an aromatic low-growing hedge or planted in mixed or shrub borders, tubs or containers. They also make ideal companions for other silver-leaved plants and herbs, where they blend to create a Mediterranean look.

TIP
Don't be too quick to deadhead lavender – goldfinches and other seed-eaters will happily devour the seeds from autumn onwards.

Rose hips (*Rosa* spp.)

Flowering time:
Mid-summer,
followed by fruit
in autumn

When to plant:
Late autumn to
late winter

Height:
Up to 2.5m (8ft),
depending on
the species

Spread:
Up to 2.5m (8ft),
depending on
the species

Hardiness:
Completely hardy

Species roses include many plants of real worth to the wildlife garden. The majority of these are vigorous, hardy shrubs that sport large, single, surprisingly fragrant flowers during the summer months. These in turn are followed by juicy red hips that often remain on the plant well into the autumn.

Single rose flowers are a real favourite with bees, flies and beetles, all visiting for both the abundant pollen and often copious nectar. The hips that follow are popular with birds, small mammals and several species of gall wasps.

Roses generally grow best on any fertile, well-drained soil in full sun, although most tolerate a degree of partial shade. The more vigorous species can be invasive in a shrub border if not controlled, although they are useful additions to mixed hedges, where the arching stems may 'ramble' freely.

TIP
Be careful when pruning roses, as birds like to use the thorny branches as protection when nesting.

Rowan/mountain ash (*Sorbus aucuparia*)

Flowering time:
Late spring, followed by fruit from late summer onwards

When to plant:
Late autumn to late winter

Height:
Variable, up to 15m (50ft), but often smaller

Spread:
Up to 7m (22ft)

Hardiness:
Extremely hardy

Rowan is a hardy little native tree, often found at high altitudes, hence its other common name of mountain ash. In gardens it is popular due to its moderate size, prettily divided leaves and bunches of white flowers followed by red berries.

The abundant, nectar-rich flowers are extremely popular with insects, including hoverflies and bees. Starlings, finches, waxwings, thrushes and even the occasional spotted flycatcher will flock to eat the berries, and the darker these are, the more attractive they prove. The leaves are eaten by several moth caterpillars, including those of brimstones and orange underwings.

All rowan needs to succeed in the garden is a humus-rich, and ideally lime-free soil – provided it is not prone to water-logging. Its relatively compact habit means that it fits well into even quite small gardens, either as a free-standing tree or a bright addition to a mixed border.

TIP
Being tolerant of pollution, this tree is ideal for urban settings.

Euonymus (*Euonymus fortunei*)

Flowering time:
Insignificant flowers in summer, followed by bright fruit capsules in autumn

When to plant:
Autumn to early spring

Height:
Up to 5m (15ft) as a climber

Spread:
Indefinite

Hardiness:
Completely hardy

This small evergreen shrub is widely planted in towns and gardens, where it is used as ground cover or as a slow-growing climber. Many cultivars exist, most of which have varying degrees of leaf variegation – and all of which tend to tinge pink or bronze in the wintertime. The rather inconspicuous flowers produced in late spring are followed by pink fruit with orange seeds that tend to persist until late into the autumn.

Euonymus provides light cover for roosting birds, and the flowers, though insignificant, provide a source of nectar for insects. The fruit borne in the autumn are eaten by birds, particularly starlings, sparrows, woodpigeons, garden warblers and finches. The thick evergreen foliage also provides good winter protection for overwintering populations of ladybirds and other insects.

Euonymus is tolerant of most soils, and this, combined with the attractive evergreen foliage, means it has become a popular ornamental plant in gardens and parks.

TIP
The whole plant is mildly toxic and the bright-coloured seeds may prove tempting to children, so be careful if planting in a family garden.

Rambling roses (*Rosa* spp.)

Flowering time:
Summer
When to plant:
Late autumn to
late winter
Height:
Up to 8m (25ft)
Spread:
4m (12 ft)
Hardiness:
Completely hardy

Rambling roses are deservedly popular in gardens due to their ability to quickly cover walls, fences and garden structures. Among these, *Rosa* 'Wedding Day', pictured here, is an excellent choice for wildlife, as its attractive, single, pure white, fragrant flowers, which are borne in umbels in early summer, are popular with visiting pollinators.

Bees are attracted to the flowers, seeking pollen as well as nectar. Once they mature, the orange clusters of hips that follow are eaten by small mammals and birds. Many insects, including ladybirds and lacewings, will overwinter among the stems and foliage.

Rambling roses will tolerate a range of soils, as long as they are free draining. They do best planted in full sun in a sheltered location.

TIP
Try growing a red or pink large-flowered clematis with single blooms up through the rose for added interest and to extend the flowering season.

Ivy (*Hedera* spp.)

Flowering time:
Late summer to autumn

When to plant:
Anytime, particularly autumn and spring

Height:
10m (30ft) as a climber

Spread:
10m (30ft) as a climber, indefinite as ground cover

Hardiness:
Completely hardy

Ivy is a familiar sight across the British countryside, as well as in gardens. It is available in many varieties, and whether green or variegated it grows as a vigorous, evergreen, self-clinging climber. It has two distinct phases: juvenile and adult. The main difference between the two is found in the leaf shape: the juvenile leaves are small and five-lobed, whereas the adult foliage is diamond shaped.

The flowers provide late nectar for bees, hoverflies and butterflies, including our native red admiral (pictured), and the flower buds are eaten by the caterpillar of the holly blue butterfly. The berries are valuable winter food for birds, particularly thrushes and finches, while wrens and blackbirds nest in the foliage.

Ivy is easily grown in almost all soil types or situations – as a result it is sometimes difficult to control. It makes excellent coverage for walls or sheds and is frequently used as ground cover. The berries that appear in late autumn are poisonous, however, and the foliage can be an intestinal and external skin irritant, so it is a good idea to wear gloves when pruning or handling ivy.

TIP
Due to its vigorous growth, ivy is ideal for planting over unsightly walls or buildings that you want to hide quickly.

Hops (*Humulus lupulus* 'Aureus')

Flowering time:
Summer
When to plant:
Late autumn to
early spring
Height:
6m (20ft)
Spread:
Up to 6m (20ft)
Hardiness:
Completely hardy

Hop plants are herbaceous, twining climbers with hairy, rough stems and deeply divided, three–five-lobed leaves. There are separate male and female plants and it is the female that is grown ornamentally. Female plants produce green-yellow hop fruits that hang in clusters during autumn.

The caterpillars of the comma butterfly and the buttoned snout moth feed on the leaves, while small birds use the dried hop fruits as nesting material. Left uncut, the stems will harbour overwintering insects.

Hops thrive in full sun or semi-shade in deep, fertile, well-drained soil. They are traditionally used in the production of beer, but in the garden they are brilliant for clothing a pergola or arch or for screening a fence or wall.

Although growth each year is rampant, all top growth will die off in winter. Old stems can then be pruned away at soil level, allowing new shoots to develop in spring which will quickly cover their support.

TIP
Despite their obvious charm, hops can be a little bland, so try combining them with a purple, single-flowered clematis to create a striking colour combination.

Food for thought

You will need:
■ Wire, glass or hopper feeder
■ Nails and hammer
■ Bird seed or nuts

Feeding, far from being simply a way to help birds through the winter months, can be beneficial throughout the year. The food that we provide can have a very positive influence on the bird populations using our gardens, helping them through the lean times of winter and supporting adult birds foraging for their young.

Many birds that were once common are in decline as their natural habitats disappear, and the efforts of gardeners can do a great deal to help them. Feeders come in a variety of forms, the most popular are: wire feeders – usually filled with peanuts, they help prevent birds choking on whole nuts; glass feeders – usually filled with mixed seed, accessible through a series of small hoppers in the side; hopper feeders – used for a range of foods, including seed and live food and may be designed to favour smaller songbirds.

When they feed, birds are very vulnerable to ambush by predators, so feeders are best positioned in an open site where birds can see anything approaching. Also ensure there is cover such as trees or hedges nearby, to allow them to escape. Avoid placing feeders near nest boxes, as the busy atmosphere can put other birds off nesting.

TIP
Once you start feeding birds, it is important that you keep it up, as they soon come to depend on it.

Squirrel off!

You will need:
■ Feeders
with a cage or
sliding cover
■ Nails and
hammer

Food put out for the birds often proves an irresistible temptation for other garden visitors. Squirrels are one such animal, and despite the fact that their antics are amusing to watch, they can often damage the feeder in their rush to get the seeds out.

While there are numerous designs available, the most common squirrel-proof feeders consist of a large, tough, metal cage around a conventional seed feeder, preventing all but the smaller wild birds from reaching the food. The cage is essentially bite-proof and has the advantage of offering more perching areas and some of the larger ones also give the birds protection inside the cage from cats and predatory hawks.

Before you become tempted to provide a separate 'squirrel feeder' nearby, however, you should consider that grey squirrels are an introduced species that, despite their cute appearance, can often attack and kill young songbird nestlings. Furthermore, feeding them can make them less wary and even aggressive towards humans.

TIP
Squirrels and magpies are predators of young nesting chicks, so discourage their visits by using a squirrel-proof cage. These will also stop larger birds like magpies accessing the food.

Window on the world

You will need:
- Bird table
- Pole
- Window feeder
- Bird seed

Window feeders are an exciting way to view birds. By bringing them almost into the house, close observation of their feeding habits is easy.

These feeders are mounted directly on to the window. However, birds often tend to be wary of this type of feeder, as it brings them so apparently close to people. If your garden birds are not used to your presence, they may need a little gentle persuasion before they will use it.

The best way to do this is to set up a familiar bird table close to the house, and mount the window feeder on a pole in the ground nearby, so they get used to feeding from it. Once the birds 'trust' the feeder, you can progressively move the pole and feeder closer to the house, before finally attaching it to the window.

TIP
Small children often find feeding birds especially entertaining, so get them involved in putting out the food for them.

Fat lot of goodness

You will need:

- Block of lard or suet
- Mixing bowl
- Saucepan
- Spoon
- String or twine
- Some old yogurt pots
- Various seeds and nuts

Birds often need a good deal of oily food to help them survive the winter, so a mixture of protein-rich seeds and vegetable fat makes an ideal dietary supplement. Fat cakes are very easy to make and will keep your garden visitors well fed through the lean winter months.

Start by melting some hard vegetable fat in a pan, before adding the dry mix. Stir in two parts of dry seed mixture to every one part of fat, until the mixture sticks together. Pierce the bottom of a yogurt pot and thread a length of string through, before packing the pot with the warm fat mixture. Leave a good trail of the string coming out at both ends of the pot.

Then place the pots in a fridge to set, and once hardened, cut and peel away the pot. Tie both ends of the string together and hang the cake from the branch of a tree or shrub.

TIP
You can also add other foodstuffs, such as wild bird seed mix, currants/sultanas, oats, bread/cake crumbs, grated cheese or peanuts.

from
£799
CARIBBEAN
ALL INCLUSIVE
10 nights 1st class hotel
Breezes Jibacoa: beautiful, tranquil setting, just an hour away from the Cuban capital, Havana. Between long white sand beach and green hills, in scenic countryside, on the island's north coast.
My nominations for the worst in-flight meals
Worst short haul
Airlines, cabin

Natural born feeders

You will need:

- Block of lard or suet
- Mixing bowl
- Saucepan
- Spoon
- String, twine or wire
- Pine cones
- Various seeds and nuts

Fatty food supplements help many birds through the lean times of winter, and these easy-to-make pine cone feeders are not only cheap but also use only natural products. They are perfect for small, agile birds such as blue tits, which will reward you by eating garden pests all summer long.

Chop up some seeds, nuts and fruit into small pieces and melt some hard vegetable fat in a pan. Add the dry mix using two parts of dry material to every one part of fat, until the mixture sticks together. Push the warm mix into the spaces between the scales of a large pine cone, making sure it is tightly packed in.

Hang the cones out throughout the winter, tying the finished feeders on to the branch of a tree with some twine.

TIP
Place the cones 120–150cm (4–5ft) high and away from dense cover, to prevent predators ambushing the birds.

Christmas is for birds too

You will need:

- Various sprigs of greenery with berries attached
- Dried fruit, such as apple slices or apricots
- Floristry wire
- Wire or wicker wreath frame
- Bracket
- Some pine cone feeders (see page 82)

Making treats for the birds is a fun family activity that can range from simple titbits to more elaborate adornments hung around the garden. Why not give your own unique seasonal greeting to the birds by making a wildlife-friendly Christmas wreath?

The best way to make your wreath is to use a pre-formed wire or wicker frame to give it the shape it needs. Using floristry wire, attach the branches by wrapping the wire round the frame. Overlay successive branches until the whole of the frame is hidden.

Finally, you can add to the seasonal effect by attaching some pieces of dried fruit or peanuts in their shells to the frame using some shorter lengths of wire. You can also add other food items, such as pine cones filled with fat and seeds.

TIP
If you like, add some decorative ribbon to give it a final, festive finishing touch.

Apple ring

You will need:
- Big bag of apples or other windfall fruit
- Thick-gauge floristry wire
- Wire snips and pliers
- Tree branch, bush or bracket to hang it from

Windfall apples and pears often attract crowds of hungry birds, including resident blackbirds and thrushes as well as winter visitors from Europe, such as redwings and fieldfares. Even if you don't have a fruit tree, you can supplement their diet by leaving some fruit out for them.

Apples in particular can be used to make attractive, edible tree decorations for birds. Simply thread fresh or, even better, windfall apples on to a ring of thick-gauge floristry wire to form an apple garland or wreath to hang from your tree.

You can also put slices of fruit on bird tables or shallow 'saucer-feeders' for larger birds that don't like to cling on in order to feed.

TIP
Oranges sliced in half can also be hung individually from strings, and you may like to experiment with a whole range of fruit once the birds have a taste for it.

Got it covered

You will need:

- Bird table with a roof
- Plastic sheeting
- Water-retentive matting
- Box of galvanised tacks
- About 1m (40in) of 50 x 12mm (2 x ½in) timber batten
- Screws and screwdriver
- Sedum matting
- Slow-release fertiliser

Many bird tables sold commercially have a roof, and while this can limit their value to all but smaller birds, they have great wildlife-friendly potential if you give them a living, green roof. It not only looks attractive, but can also encourage more wildlife to visit your garden.

The best plants to use are sedums, as they withstand both drought and poor soil. You can often buy ready-made sedum matting, which can simply be cut to size and rolled out. Cover the roof with some plastic sheeting, securing it with galvanised tacks. Cut some water-retentive matting and fix this over the plastic, again, securing with galvanised tacks.

Make a baton edge around the roof to hold the sedum mat in place. Then simply cut the matting to size and lay it over the roof of the bird table – it will stay in place without the need for tacking it down. Water the mat in and place the table in a sunny location.

TIP
Give the plants a boost and sprinkle the sedum mat with some slow-release fertiliser once laid out.

Swing round for supper

You will need:

- Shallow metal or plastic dish
- String, wire or hanging basket chains
- Drill and narrow drill bit
- Seeds, crushed nuts, shredded suet, dried and live mealworms or small pieces of chopped fruit

Garden bird feeders do not need to be complicated or expensive to be useful. A simple saucer feeder is very easy to make, and when hung from a branch, hook or pole will attract a wide range of birds, while allowing you to provide a variety of food items.

Drill three or four holes around the edge of a shallow metal or plastic dish and thread string or wire through each one. Add a knot below each hole to stop the string pulling through, trim each length to about twice the diameter of the dish and tie them together at the top. Drill some small drainage holes in the base of the dish to keep the food dry.

Once you have hung the feeder, it can be used for a variety of foods, including seeds, crushed nuts, shredded suet, dried and live mealworms or small pieces of chopped fruit.

TIP
Don't mix food types, and remember to wash the dish if changing from one to another.

Seeds of plenty

You will need:
- Secateurs
- Clean paper bags
- String for tying stems and hanging bags

Late summer and autumn are often a period of plenty for garden wildlife, busy enjoying the glut of food at the end of the growing season. The hungry period that follows can be hard, but you can easily help balance things out by holding some of the food back until later.

Look around your garden for plants with seedheads that birds naturally feed on, such as buddleia and lavender. Once the seeds are ripe, cut off the seedheads and shake them into a paper bag, or hang them upside down to dry with the bag loosely tied over the stem to catch the falling seeds. They will provide a welcome bonus in the hungrier months and can be an extremely cost-effective way to feed garden wildlife.

In the case of larger seeds, such as sunflowers, these can be separated from the heads by hand and stored in a cool dry place.

TIP
You can also remove the whole flower head, so that it can be hung complete at a later date and act as a feeder in its own right.

Cracking good dinner

You will need:
■ Wooden posts, gnarled tree trunk or old cracked log
■ Shredded suet
■ Mixture of additional food, such as oil-rich seeds, dried mealworms and dried fruit
■ Dibber or pointed stick

When feeding garden birds, it is important that this does not adversely affect their normal behaviour patterns. Many agile birds, such as tits, nuthatches, woodpeckers, tree-creepers, and even wrens, like to cling on to old craggy branches and trunks to find food morsels hidden in the cracks.

To help these species, you can try to mimic their natural food sources by filling any holes and cracks that you find in wooden posts, gnarled tree trunks or even a suspended log, with fatty foods. A mixture of suet, oil-rich seeds, dried mealworms and even dried fruit is particularly enticing for them.

Foods based on suet will be enjoyed by many species, but avoid polyunsaturated fats, as they don't really offer the birds the high levels of energy they require in winter.

TIP
To reduce the risk of birds choking on dried fruit or nuts, press them tightly into cracks so they can't be pulled out whole.

A clean sweep

You will need:
- Pot brush or other similar scrubbing brush
- Paint-scraping knife
- Some fresh water
- Detergent
- Unfragranced disinfectant

Bird tables are a good way of feeding birds a whole range of foods. They also have the advantage of being off the ground, thereby reducing the chances of mice and rats getting at the food first.

A bird table is ideally suited to serving up high-energy foods, including seeds, live food, grated cheese, breadcrumbs, cooked rice and pasta, fat or rind from meat, as well as dried or fresh fruit. The range of foodstuffs placed on a bird table, however, means that wooden tables in particular need regular cleaning, ideally every couple of weeks, or more frequently if they become very dirty.

Clean the surface with a hose and scrubbing brush to remove old food, droppings and mould. Then spray with an unfragranced disinfectant, ideally the sort designed for cleaning pet cages or aviaries.

TIP
When choosing a bird table, remember that the simplest design is usually the best, and often proves to be the easiest to clean and maintain.

Summer salad for butterflies

You will need:

■ Small breakfast bowl or deep saucer (15–20cm/ 6–8in diameter is ideal)
■ Set of hanging basket chains
■ Adhesive putty or tape to prevent the chains slipping
■ Mixture of fully ripe fruits, such as bananas, oranges, apples, strawberries, etc

Butterflies normally find enough food in the flowers that they visit to keep them going, although they will readily feast on a combination of ripe fruit and fruit juices if it's offered to them. A butterfly feeder is quite simple to make, consisting of a shallow dish suspended on thin chains and filled with a selection of chopped fruit pieces.

Choose ripe fruit, as this will produce the greatest aroma, and in a range of colours, as butterflies are attracted by both bright colours and sweet smells. Use large chunks to create big blocks of colour that butterflies can see easily. These will also provide good landing spots.

Hang the feeder no more than waist high, in a nice sunny spot away from the house – in case it attracts wasps – using the hanging basket chains. It can be left there for two or three days before the fruit will need to be replaced.

TIP
Add some fruit juice, ideally from a pungent fruit such as pineapple, to keep the fruit pieces moist and to help release their sugars.

Liquid refreshment

You will need:
- Large saucer
- Some muddy water
- Some rounded stones

While we may go to great lengths to provide butterflies with nectar and shelter, we often overlook one aspect of their feeding. Nectar (or fruit juice), may be rich in sugar and water, but it rarely provides all the minerals that the insects need, especially at the times when they are producing eggs.

You can easily provide a mineral-rich 'drinking-place' by simply leaving a saucer of muddy water on the ground, in full sun, near a butterfly feeder or some of their favourite flowers. Place a few rounded stones into the saucer to give the butterflies a dry place to land so they can sip the water.

To complete your butterfly habitat, place several large, flat, dark-coloured stones or rocks nearby in full sun. Butterflies are real sun lovers, and in order to be able to fly they must warm up. Rocks are ideal basking sites, and you will see butterflies using them in the morning or after a dull period in the day.

TIP
Mixing a little weak sugar water and animal manure into the muddy water will make an even tastier, nutritious drink for insects.

Get bogged down

- Spade
- Well-rotted garden compost
- Well-worked (crumbly) garden soil
- Flexible butyl or PVC garden pond liner
- Enough stones or rubble to cover the base
- Hosepipe
- Range of bog plants

Many species of plants and animals naturally live in marshy areas, and a bog garden is an ideal way to help these. The trick is to construct an area that has permanently waterlogged soil. The easiest way to do this is to use the same type of flexible liner that is used when making a pond.

Dig a hole at least 60cm (2ft) in depth and line this with the pond liner. Pierce the liner a couple of times to prevent the bog garden becoming stagnant and smelly, before placing a layer of rubble or large stones over it. Fill the hole with a mixture of crumbly soil and well-rotted garden compost.

Choose plants for the bog that like wet conditions, and species that will not grow too big for the setting. Suitable bog plants include yellow flag iris (*Iris pseudacorus*), marsh marigold (*Caltha palustris*), hemp agrimony (*Eupatorium cannabinum*), purple loosestrife (*Lythrum salicaria*), ragged robin (*Lychnis flos-cuculi*), dwarf bulrush (*Typha minima*). Once planted, fill the area with water and keep topping it up – particularly during spells of dry weather – so the area stays marshy.

TIP
It is much easier to plant up before watering the area.

Hogging the limelight

You will need to:
- Piles of branches and leaves in sheltered corners
- Leave out plenty of their preferred food
- Check piles of leaves or branches carefully before moving them

Hedgehogs are surprisingly common, even in quite built-up areas. Although they are rarely seen, being shy and mostly nocturnal, if you keep your garden wildlife friendly it will raise your chances of catching a glimpse of one of these peculiar and reclusive native mammals.

In order to encourage hedgehogs into your garden, you'll need to lure in plenty of their preferred food items: insects, worms, woodlice and other small invertebrates. Gardens are ideal hunting grounds, and an abundance of food limits their need for a very large territory, meaning they may even take up permanent residence.

Give them plenty of tall vegetation to hide in, and build up piles of old branches and leaves in sheltered corners for them to sleep or hibernate in. Make ramps out of any sunken areas and ponds, or up steps, to ensure they don't become stranded. Avoid using insecticides, both because they reduce the abundance of their prey species and because hedgehogs accumulate these poisons to lethal levels over time.

TIP
Supplement hedgehogs' natural diet in autumn to help them accumulate fat before hibernating. Feed them tinned cat or dog food, dry dog food and bacon rind, but not milk or bread in large amounts as these can cause diarrhoea. Put out fresh water with any food.

Save our robins

You will need to:
■ Leave out
kitchen scraps
■ Encourage
insects to
hibernate to
provide a winter
food larder
■ Make leaf piles

The robin is a familiar garden bird that feeds mainly on insects and other small invertebrates, eating vegetable matter only in the cooler months when insects are scarce. They are important pest controllers and helping them will aid the whole health of the garden in the long term.

Like many over-wintering birds, robins face a bleak prospect when temperatures drop severely. Small garden birds can actually lose up to 10 per cent of their body weight during one cold winter's night. Unless they are able to feed well every day to replenish their reserves, a prolonged cold spell can be fatal.

Although providing extra food such as mealyworms and chopped peanuts can help during these times, wild food is always best. You can also leave out meaty kitchen scraps, fat, cheese, cake or biscuit crumbs and dried fruit in the winter and early spring. Help them through the winter by making leaf piles and leaving hollow plant stems for over-wintering insects. This provides them with a perfect hunting ground, helping to reduce their dependency on human provision.

TIP
Remember that birds have a very high metabolic rate, so they must have a continuous supply of food. Once you start feeding them, don't stop, even for a couple of days.

Summer sting

You will need to:
■ Avoid using
pesticides
■ Mulch borders
with a coarse
woody compost
mix to encourage
carnivorous
beetles
■ Provide plenty
of flat-flowered
and daisy-flowered
plants

Wasps are possibly the least-loved insects that visit our gardens through the summer, yet for much of the year they are great pest controllers, eating their way through tens of thousands of garden insects each season.

Of the 25,000 wasp species, most are small, stingless and highly beneficial in terms of pest control. The adults only eat sugary food, such as nectar, and either hunt insects for their young or lay eggs in or on a host insect that is devoured by the emerging larvae.

The much-maligned 'jaspers' or 'yellow-jackets' are large, social wasps that depend on their larvae for food, exchanging insect flesh they have caught in return for sugary liquid secreted by the grubs. They generally only become a nuisance in the autumn, as the colony dies off and the adults disperse seeking sugar. This is the time when they are often encountered alongside other wasps, bees, flies and butterflies visiting nectar-rich ivy flowers.

TIP
Leave areas of long grass and thickets of vegetation whenever possible – they are ideal places for beneficial insects to gather.

Pots of colour

- Large pot
- Crocks
- Potting compost
- Selection of bright summer-flowering plants

You will be surprised just how many things you can actually grow in a pot. It is perfectly feasible to have a garden that is full of resplendent bloom and abuzz with wildlife using no more than containers.

For daytime insects, try combinations of flower shapes and bright colours with plants such as yarrow (*Achillea millefolium*), salvia, catmint (*Nepeta* x *faassenii*). This colourful display will attract a range of insects. Alternatively, try night-scented plants such as stocks (*Matthiola bicornis*), phlox (*Phlox paniculata*), tobacco plants (*Nicotiana sylvestris*) and heliotrope (*Heliotropium arborescens*), so you can enjoy their heady perfume while you watch moths gather around your pots.

Remember that the soil in a container is more free-draining than soil in borders, so the plants you grow will require a rich potting mix to be at their best. You can, of course, mix your own blend, but it is often easier to buy a proprietary brand specially mixed for the type of plants you plan to grow.

TIP
Add a handful of slow-release fertiliser and water-retaining granules to the potting compost to get the plants started and save yourself some maintenance.

Rattle and roll

You will need:

■ 1g of seed for every square metre of lawn

Yellow rattle (*Rhinanthus minor*) is a rather insignificant-looking plant, but it can be of great help when making an area of flowery grassland. It is a native annual that gains some of its nutrients from the roots of neighbouring grass plants, weakening them and allowing your flowering plants to gain a foothold.

To establish it, in the autumn simply scarify the surface of the ground by raking harshly with a fork. Make sure there are some bare patches so that the seed will be in contact with the soil. Sow fresh seed thinly – 1g per square metre. Don't cover the seed, just press it down with your feet or with a roller.

Keep the grass short until the beginning of March. After this, don't cut the grass until the end of July to allow the yellow rattle to flower and set seed, thereby spreading. You can sow the seed of other flowering plants at the same time, but it is often better to add them as small plants having been raised in small containers known as 'plugs' or 'thumb-pots'.

TIP
Sowing from October to late November helps plants establish good roots and makes for stronger plants the following summer.

Natural selection

You will need to:
■ Choose a range
of species
■ Plant them away
from busy areas

Animals, like humans, must have their basic requirements satisfied in order to survive. Food is probably the single most important element that you must include in your wildlife garden. Even the smallest window box on an upstairs balcony can provide a 'café' where visiting wildlife can stop and refuel.

The real trick to feeding garden wildlife naturally is to make sure that you provide food over as long a period as possible. So try to choose a range of species that provide various food types over different months. Consider carefully when they will be most useful.

For instance, choose shrubs that carry berries over a long period, and remember that spring is a crucial time when there are often few berries available in natural habitats. Go for a range of flower shapes, scents and colours, choosing them carefully so something is available for visiting wildlife all through the year.

TIP
Don't plant berry-bearing plants beside patios or paths, if you want to avoid 'treading' the berries into the house.

Make a splash

You will need to:
■ Change the water regularly to prevent the spread of diseases
■ Use pure water, or use tap water that has been boiled and left to stand for a few hours before using

Birds, and other animals, need a reasonably clean water supply at all times – ideally a shallow dish or 'bird bath' for bathing in as well as drinking from.

A bird bath has the advantage over garden ponds that you can change the water regularly to minimise the risk of spreading diseases. If placed on the ground, it will also provide clean water for other animals, such as hedgehogs.

Water is especially welcome on a cold, frosty morning when natural sources may be frozen. While the prospect of going out on icy winter mornings with a kettle of hot water to defrost the bird bath might seem unappealing, it can be vital for animals desperate for a drink.

TIP
If the water in your bird bath tends to turn green, never add salt or chemicals. Instead, change the water regularly and place the bird bath out of direct sunlight.

Leaves of gold

- Plenty of damp leaves collected as soon as they have fallen
- Old compost sacks
- Garden fork
- Some twine or wire

Turning fallen leaves into compost is a cheap, easy, and environmentally sound way of recycling them, but can also provide a small, frost-free wildlife refuge. This compost, known as leaf mould, is made from nothing more than decayed leaves, but it is pure gold – the finest soil conditioner there is.

During the winter, a leaf mould heap provides a hibernation site for amphibians and hedgehogs. It also harbours a host of insects, bacteria and fungi. These in turn provide a feast for thrushes, robins and blackbirds, as well as soil-dwelling predators, once you come to spread it over your borders.

Making leaf mould is a simple but slow process and involves gathering the wet leaves into a pile, preferably somewhere where they won't blow around, or putting them into old compost sacks tied with string and with holes punched into the base. In either case they need to be left in a cool, shady spot in the garden for about two years.

TIP
Once rotted down, spread the leaf mould over your soil to improve its structure, increase its fertility, and lock moisture into the soil – which should mean you'll need to water less.

Wriggly wonders

Earthworms are a familiar sight for gardeners, especially in soils rich in organic matter. Worms are extremely important because they help convert organic material into nutrients that plants can absorb. Their tunnelling activities loosen the soil and allow plant roots to penetrate the soil, as well as helping the passage of water and air into the soil.

Worms are an important part of many creatures' diets, including insects, amphibians, birds and mammals. In early spring, they can mean the difference between life and death to some species, particularly ground-feeding birds like blackbirds, being a good source of nutrients before seeds and berries ripen. Worm casts contain more nutrients and organic matter than the surrounding soil.

Despite preferring a damp site, worms can easily drown if the soil becomes waterlogged, and raindrops hitting the ground can cause them to make a dash for the surface. Many birds exploit this trait by lightly pecking at the ground to simulate raindrops, catching the worms as they emerge.

TIP
Unless you are growing acid-loving plants, add lime to acidic soil every four to five years to encourage worms.

Dead useful

- Some untreated stakes (ideally chestnut, as this is slow to rot)
- Mallet
- Plenty of woody branches and twigs

We usually think of hedges as being made from living plants, but they were originally constructed from cut branches and dead wood. This might seem like a strange idea, but it is an excellent way to provide shelter for a whole range of species.

This 'dead hedge' will ultimately become a habitat for many invertebrates, such as insects or spiders. It may also act as a temporary shelter for many more larger creatures.

To make this hedge, hammer a row of upright stakes into the ground. If the site is open, put a second, parallel row behind the first, or build the hedge against a freestanding wall. Then fill the space between with long, pruned branches, and fill the smaller gaps with more twiggy material. Over time, the timber will begin to rot down, so you will need to add more branches on top and replace any stakes that rot through.

TIP
As well as providing an alternative hibernation area to bonfire piles, it can also help your plants by acting as a windbreak.

Urban oasis

You will need to make sure:

- It contains plenty of diversity
- You are not too ambitious over what you include
- You leave some open spaces as well as dense cover
- That animals have food, drink and shelter as a priority

In nature, both the greatest variety and highest number of creatures are usually found where two or more habitats meet. This is because the four basic needs – food, water, shelter and breeding sites – are more likely to be met where several habitats overlap, rather than in a single one.

When you plan your garden for wildlife, whether in the town or country, try to create a space that has as much diversity as possible. A well-planned wildlife garden will naturally provide many habitats, such as hedges, shrubs, grassland, a pond and flower beds, in close proximity. Garden birds, for example, will nest or shelter in hedges, eat berries from shrubs, feed on worms in the lawn or caterpillars from flower beds, while drinking and bathing in the pond.

TIP

Work on the basics of food and water first, and then add plenty of natural shelter in order to create an oasis for a rich variety of species.

Deadwood dwelling

- Freshly cut logs with the bark on
- Untreated timber

Dead wood is an important natural habitat – many animals and some plants use it as a home, and yet more use it as a source of food. In forests, fallen wood is a natural feature, but in our tended and tidy gardens dead wood is not very common.

Making a log pile is an easy way to mimic the habitats created when trees or branches fall naturally. A well-made pile offers over-wintering sites for many amphibians and insects, and for various wood-boring beetles.

Choose a shady place and dig a trench deep enough to make sure that some of the wood is below ground level. Fill the trench with a mixture of different-sized logs. Add some leaf litter to the pile to help attract even more creatures. Avoid disturbing the pile once you have made it, and allow the wood to rot naturally. Top it up with new logs occasionally, as the old ones disintegrate.

TIP
Make the pile more of a feature by planting a range of shade-loving, native herbaceous perennials all around it.

Home-made hideaway

You will need:
- Large cardboard box
- Poster paints, brushes, rollers and a sponge
- Thin stakes
- Rubber mallet
- Craft knife
- Wire twist ties or string

Birds are naturally shy of people, as their survival depends on their alertness to danger. By watching a bird, you actually resemble a predator, stopping and looking directly at it, before slowly moving towards it. By making a temporary hide, you remove this problem and can actually get quite close to them.

A large cardboard box (the bigger the better), some poster paints, brushes, rollers and a sponge are all you need for the basic structure. Paint the box to break up the outline. Choose a site near an area frequented by birds and drive some thin stakes into the ground, attaching the 'hide' to them. Make some peep-holes in the cardboard, cutting them letter-box style, with one side of a rectangle still attached.

This hide can also be used to watch other animals and is easy to take down and store. Don't leave it out in the rain!

TIP
Cut the peep holes at varying heights to allow both children and adults to use the hide.

Snail trail

You will need:

- Durable paint, such as water-based emulsion
- Paint brushes
- Magnifying glass
- Notebook and pencil

Children love to see wildlife and get up close to garden creatures, rarely having the fearful responses so common in adults when encountering 'creepy-crawlies.' What better way of encouraging their interest than to track familiar friends around the garden.

Snails, although often hated by gardeners, are fascinating to children. Get them to put a blob of paint the shell of a snail and see where it goes each day in the garden. If you have more than one child, each one can use a different colour paint. Children will have fun looking for their snail and should encounter many other creatures during their search.

On the whole, try to avoid capturing creatures for long, as it can cause unnecessary distress. Remember also that all wild animals are just that – wild – and they can be unpredictable or even aggressive if they feel threatened. Lastly, the golden rule if you do capture an animal is to always put it back where you found it.

TIP
When tracking snails, get your children to keep a diary of their sightings.

Drawn to wildlife

You will need:
- Notebook
- Coloured pens and pencils

At one time, amateur naturalists were encouraged to collect wildflowers, butterflies, and even birds' eggs. Even today, there are still some people who take rare species from the wild, although thankfully most now take only photographs and notes. This approach is, of course, much better for wildlife and, what's more, is great fun.

Drawing an animal really helps you learn to look. Simple sketches can record the basic shapes of the animal, but you can also show the animal's movement with sequences of drawings, as well as any 'typical' poses. Never try to physically capture the animal, and be patient and practise looking at it to get the information you need.

Pay attention to eyes, wings, the number of legs, and the coloration of the animal – either sketching these or by making notes to add information. It can be a wonderful way to enhance your identification abilities and may even prove to be the start of an absorbing and rewarding hobby.

TIP
Sketch quickly to capture as much information as you can – start with simple outlines and fill colours in later.

Forget-me-not (*Myosotis arvensis*)

Flowering time:
- Spring to early summer

When to plant:
- Autumn or late winter

Height:
- 15–30cm (6–12in) or more

Spread:
- 30cm (12in) or more

Hardiness:
- Completely hardy

Field forget-me-not is a pretty annual (or sometimes biennial) that sports bright blue to dark purple flowers from spring through to early summer, followed by a healthy abundance of seeds.

Bumblebees seek out the flowers in spring for pollen and nectar. Occasionally butterflies will come to drink the nectar. In the autumn, birds such as chaffinches, linnets and a number of finches, visit the plant to feast on the seeds.

This forget-me-not will grow in sun or semi-shade and likes a fertile, well-drained soil. It is an excellent plant for naturalising in a wild garden, where it rapidly provides a splash of colour after the dull winter months. When planted alongside wallflowers, species tulips or pansies, it gives a wonderful spring display. Many colourful cultivars of forget-me-not have been bred, and these are extensively used for spring bedding displays in more formal settings.

TIP
Allow forget-me-nots to set seed to give you more plants the following year and to provide food for birds.

Pansies (*Viola* spp.)

Flowering time:
- Spring to autumn

When to plant:
- Autumn or spring

Height:
- To 12cm (5in)

Spread:
- To 30cm (1ft)

Hardiness:
- Completely hardy

Pansies are pretty flowers descended from wild counterparts that grow naturally in open grassland, where they bloom from spring onwards. Many cultivars have been raised, but it is the smaller-flowered forms that prove most useful to wildlife.

The flowers of pansies are especially favoured by bumblebees in spring – the tufted blooms of the smaller-flowered types are perfect for them to land on. The seeds are eaten by several species of birds, including bullfinches and coal tits.

Pansies are best grown in full sun or light shade, and prefer a light, free-draining but moist soil. They prove to be ideal little plants for using as spring bedding, or as fillers in a border, where their pretty little 'faces' pop up among other plants.

TIP
The large showy-flowered types are impossible for bees to land on and are therefore best avoided.

Wallflowers (*Erysimum* spp.)

Flowering time:
- Late winter to early summer

When to plant:
- Autumn

Height:
- 25–80cm (10–32in)

Spread:
- 30–40cm (12–16in)

Hardiness:
- Completely hardy

A familiar sight in spring bedding displays, where it is treated as a biennial, this sweetly scented, sturdy little plant is actually a short-lived perennial. It is best grown in full sun, but will grow in dappled shade in any well-drained soil, performing best in alkaline conditions.

The sweetly-scented, nectar-rich flowers from late winter to early spring; provide a welcome early source of food for many insects. They are especially attractive to bees, who take both pollen and nectar, as well as butterflies emerging from hibernation in spring.

Its popularity as spring bedding is mainly due to the reliability of its flowering, but also the great range of heights and colours that many of the cultivars provide.

TIP
Wallflowers will readily establish in old masonry walls, or other dry, stony sites, where they often naturalise quickly.

Foxglove (*Digitalis purpurea*)

Flowering time:
- Late spring to early summer

When to plant:
- Late summer to late autumn or early spring

Height:
- 1–2m (3–6ft)

Spread:
- To 60cm (2ft)

Hardiness:
- Completely hardy

With its tall spikes of tubular white, pink or purple flowers, the foxglove is a familiar sight in gardens from late spring through to early summer. It is commonly grown as a biennial, although it often proves to be a short-lived perennial that, given the opportunity, naturalises readily.

Foxgloves are an important plant for bumblebees seeking the copious nectar, while fallen seeds are eaten by birds foraging in the border.

Being woodland plants, foxgloves are best grown in semi-shade, on moist but well-drained soil that is rich in humus. They are equally at home in full sun, however, and look best when planted randomly throughout a mixed or herbaceous border or – if space permits – in large drifts under trees. The whole plant is very poisonous though, and you should always wash your hands after handling it.

TIP
Don't cut back these plants in autumn – leave the old, hollow stems for insects to overwinter in.

Honesty (*Lunaria annua*)

Flowering time:
■ Spring and summer, followed by seed pods in summer to autumn

When to plant:
■ Late summer to late autumn or early spring

Height:
■ To 90cm (36in)

Spread:
■ To 30cm (12in)

Hardiness:
■ Completely hardy

While the beautiful white to purple flowers that grace this biennial plant in late spring and summer are a major plus, it is the round, papery seed heads that are most easily recognised. They dry to an attractive silvery grey colour and are widely used in floral arrangements.

The scented flowers are very attractive to butterflies and moths, as well as bees, which in turn attract birds to feed on them. The leaves of honesty are a larval food plant of the orange-tip butterfly, and the mature seeds are quickly eaten by overwintering birds, especially bullfinches.

Honesty grows in just about any well-drained soil, in full sun or dappled shade, although to attract the greatest number of insects it is best planted in full sun. It is an ideal candidate to brighten up shady corners and looks great among shrubs and trees or naturalised in a wild garden.

TIP
If you want to collect seedheads for flower arranging, try to take only the minimum of stems, as birds love them over winter.

Borage (*Borago officinalis*)

Flowering time:
- Spring to late summer

When to plant:
- Sow seed in-situ or in small pots in spring
- Plant out pot-sown plants in mid-spring

Height:
- 60cm (24in)

Spread:
- 45cm (18in)

Hardiness:
- Completely hardy

This familiar annual herb is best known for its beautiful, star-shaped, sky-blue flowers, which often have tinges of white and pink.

Both the blue and white forms of borage are among the best plants for attracting a wide range of bee species. Chief among these are honey and bumblebees, which benefit from the abundant nectar they produce.

Borage thrives in a warm, sunny location on free-draining, fertile soil, where it will self-seed, returning year after year. It is an ideal addition to annual or mixed borders, or can be dotted around vegetable gardens to encourage pollinators. If your soil is rich and moist, the closely related *Borago pygmaea* is a short-lived perennial that prefers damper conditions.

TIP
As well as attracting wildlife, the edible flowers can be picked and used in salads or frozen in ice cubes, then served up in summer drinks.

Sunflowers (*Helianthus* spp.)

Flowering time:
- Summer

When to plant:
- Sow seed in-situ or in small pots in spring
- Plant out pot-sown plants in mid-spring

Height:
- Up to 5m (16ft)

Spread:
- To 60cm (2ft)

Hardiness:
- Hardy, but best started indoors in cooler locations

It's easy to see why sunflowers are a great favourite with children, when they bear their huge, yellow, daisy-like flowers in summer. Many cultivars are available, offering gardeners a range of colours as well as tall, medium and dwarf sizes.

Honey bees and bumblebees love both the nectar and pollen produced by sunflowers, which also attract the occasional butterfly. When the flowers fade, the oily seeds that follow are a real favourite with a range of seed-eating birds, including collared doves, greenfinches, nuthatches, long-tailed tits, cross bills and bramblings.

For the best results, grow your sunflowers in well-drained, fertile soil in full sun. Plant them in large groups or dot them among other plants. If space is limited, dwarf varieties can be used in tubs and window boxes.

Allow plants to set seed and die down naturally in summer before clearing away their remains. Fallen seed will usually germinate in autumn to form a green carpet of seedlings, and these will then flower the following year.

TIP
Tall varieties need staking as they grow, so shorter ones are best for windy sites.

Poached egg plant *(Limnanthes douglasii)*

Flowering time:
- Summer to autumn

When to plant:
- Sow seed in-situ in spring
- Sow in mid-autumn in mild locations

Height:
- To 15cm (6in)

Spread:
- To 15cm (6in)

Hardiness:
- Completely hardy

This small, fast-growing, hardy annual plant produces brilliantly eye-catching, lightly scented, cup-shaped white flowers with yellow centres from summer to autumn. These leave no doubt as to how it gained its common name of poached egg plant.

The brightly coloured flowers are an excellent nectar source for bees. They also attract an abundance of hoverflies, the larvae of which are great predators of garden pests such as aphids.

Poached egg plants are easy to grow in full sun on any moderately fertile soil. They are best sown in their final position and make ideal edging plants for a mixed or herbaceous border. They will also grow between the cracks in a paved path or patio, or at the base of a south-facing hedge, where they will provide a welcome splash of colour throughout the summer.

TIP
Poached egg plants will appreciate some added organic matter to help retain moisture in the soil.

Heliotrope (*Heliotropium arborescens*)

Flowering time:
■ Summer
When to plant:
■ Early summer
Height:
■ 1.2m (4ft) in
open ground;
45cm (18in) in
containers
Spread:
■ 30–45cm
(12–18in)
Hardiness:
■ Tender shrub;
usually treated
as a half-hardy
annual

Heliotrope has a delicious fragrance that you can often smell before you spot the small, tubular, white or purple to pink flowers. Indeed, the scent of this plant, which is reminiscent of sweet marshmallows, is hugely attractive to many night-flying insects.

Bees and bumblebees seek out the nectar-rich flowers, and their tubular shape makes the nectar accessible to many species of butterfly, too, such as the comma, painted lady and colourful peacock. Daytime- flying moths, such as the humming bird hawk moth, also find the nectar irresistible, as do many of the night-flying species.

Naturally a tender shrub, it is treated as a half-hardy annual due to its poor frost hardiness. It needs a sheltered spot in full sun or dappled shade, on a fertile, well-drained soil.

TIP
Plant some near the house so you can enjoy their sweet fragrance in the evening.

Pot marigold (*Calendula officinalis*)

Flowering time:
■ Spring to autumn

When to plant:
■ Sow seed
in-situ in spring
to mid-autumn

Height:
■ To 70cm (28in)

Spread:
■ To 45cm (18in)

Hardiness:
■ Completely
hardy

These familiar, brightly coloured, hardy annuals are a real winner with both gardeners and wildlife alike. The stunning disc-shaped daisy flowers are borne freely from spring to early autumn and range from yellow and brown through to orange. They are held high above the strongly aromatic, pale green leaves.

Marigolds are a favourite with hoverflies (whose larvae provide a free 'pest-control service'), honey bees and bumblebees, and even the occasional butterfly. Always plant single-flowered cultivars or the straight species to encourage wildlife. Avoid double-flowered cultivars such as 'Art Shades' or the popular 'Fiesta' series, as these offer little pollen and nectar, and ultimately have little value to wildlife.

Marigolds thrive in full sun on well-drained soils. For flowers in spring, sow seed in autumn where they are to flower, otherwise sow in mid spring for summer blooms.

TIP
They look great anywhere in the garden that you want a lively splash of colour.

Poppies (*Papaver* spp.)

Flowering time:
■ Late spring
to summer
When to plant:
■ Sow seed in-situ
from mid-autumn
to spring
Height:
■ To 1.2m (4ft)
Spread:
■ To 30cm (12in)
Hardiness:
■ Completely
hardy

This familiar annual bears large, mauve, red or white blooms in late spring to summer. They are commonly seen on waste ground as well as in gardens, where they have escaped and become naturalised, particularly in urban areas.

All poppy species are popular with insects, the flowers attracting honey bees and bumblebees, hoverflies and the occasional butterfly. The nutritious seeds are eaten by sparrows, siskins, linnets dunnocks and a number of finches.

Annual poppies are easy to grow in full sun on any well-drained soil, into which the seeds are sown direct in early spring. These plants provide a welcome splash of colour in the garden. They are best regarded as poisonous, though, given that cultivars of *Papaver somniferum* are actually decorative forms of the opium poppy, although they carry no real risk when grown simply as an ornamental plant.

TIP
Let poppies self-seed among
other border plants for a
display the following year.

Alliums (*Allium* spp.)

Flowering time:
■ Late spring to mid-summer
When to plant:
■ Plant bulbs in autumn
Height:
■ To 60cm (2ft) or more, depending on the species
Spread:
■ 5–20cm (2–8in), depending on the species
Hardiness:
■ Completely hardy

Essentially a sort of spring-flowering, ornamental onion, alliums are wonderfully architectural plants in the garden. Their round flower heads are made up of smaller, star-shaped, individual flowers, in colours from purple to white. They are also great providers of nectar for bees and many other types of insect.

Alliums are popular with bees, early butterflies and many other insects, drawn by the copious nectar.

Alliums thrive on well-drained soils in sunny locations and are established as bulbs rather than seed or plants. Dot them among other border plants so the flower heads 'float' above the surrounding vegetation. Always leave these on the plant after flowering. During the winter months, they will provide hibernation sites for insects, while extending the plants' ornamental value, especially when laced with frost.

TIP
Choosing a range of allium species will extend flowering over a prolonged period and ensure a steady supply of nectar.

Yarrow (*Achillea millefolium*)

Flowering time:
- Summer

When to plant:
- Mid-autumn or early spring

Height:
- To 75cm (30in) or more

Spread:
- To 60cm (2ft) or more

Hardiness:
- Completely hardy

Yarrow is a perfect choice for the wildlife garden, with graceful, upright stems culminating in large, long-lasting, flat-topped flower heads during the summer. These vary in colour between species and cultivars and can be white, yellow, pink or cerise-red, and provide an ideal landing platform for many visiting insects seeking nectar.

Hoverflies swarm to the nectar in the flat flower heads. Bumblebees and numerous other species of insects are also frequent visitors. These in turn attract insect-eating birds, and the seed heads attract seed-eating birds, in particular house sparrows, tits and chaffinches, in late summer and autumn.

Yarrow is easy to grow and trouble free, needing no more than a sunny site on any good, well-drained soil. It is a great addition to a herbaceous border; the broad flower heads providing contrasting shapes within a display.

TIP
Yarrow looks stunning when planted in large drifts.

Scabious (*Scabiosa* spp.)

Flowering time:
■ Mid- to late summer

When to plant:
■ Mid-autumn or early spring

Height:
■ To 60cm (2ft)

Spread:
■ 60cm (2ft)

Hardiness:
■ Completely hardy

Scabious is a wonderfully showy plant. It produces large, lilac-blue flower heads with pincushion-like centres in summer through to late autumn. These seem to float over the low-growing foliage, dancing and swaying in even the lightest breeze. It is also in bloom for a long time – a real bonus for wildlife and gardeners alike.

All scabious species are popular with insects, and are particular favourites of butterflies and bees. This is due not only to the large amount of nectar produced, but also because the plant's long flowering period maintains the feast for many weeks.

This plant is an ideal choice for a dry, sunny spot, and although it is not overly fussy about the soil type, it will struggle in acidic or waterlogged conditions. It is a wonderful addition to the front of a herbaceous or mixed border, where you can really appreciate its subtle charms. It can also be naturalised on dry, grassy banks.

TIP
There are numerous varieties of scabious available, so you should be able to find a colour to suit any planting scheme.

Phlox (*Phlox* spp.)

Flowering time:
- Summer to mid-autumn

When to plant:
- Autumn or spring

Height:
- 1.2m (4ft)

Spread:
- 60–100cm (24–39in)

Hardiness:
- Completely hardy

Phlox ranks among the true aristocrats of the late-summer garden. Its tall stems are topped with large, round heads of tubular, scented, white, purple or pink flowers creating a glorious splash of colour. The flowers are rich in nectar and are an important source of food for a whole range of insects.

Butterflies are the most striking of the daytime visitors, lured by the sweetly scented flowers and the promise of nectar. Hawk moths may be seen hovering around the flowers from late afternoon until dusk, and then numerous other species of night-flying moths will join them.

Summer phlox will grow in almost any soil, but will perform best on rich, moist but free-draining soil in full sun or semi-shade. Its height proves useful in herbaceous or mixed borders.

TIP
Plant phlox alongside other butterfly-attracting species, such as scabious and verbena, to create a colourful butterfly border.

Bergamot (*Monarda* spp.)

Flowering time:
■ From mid- to late summer

When to plant:
■ Early to mid-spring

Height:
■ 90cm (36in) or more

Spread:
■ 45cm (18in)

Hardiness:
■ Completely hardy

Bergamot, or bee balm as it is sometimes known, is a striking addition to any garden. Its rounded, disc-shaped flower heads are adorned with bright crimson, tubular flowers. As the name suggests, it is a superb plant for attracting bees, although it often attracts a whole host of other insects too.

The nectar-rich flowers attract hummingbird hawk moths, which hover in front of the flowers and sip the nectar. Leave the plant's old flower stems in place over winter and all the small crevices and hollows will provide an over-wintering site for small insects such as ladybirds.

Bergamot is not particular about its soil type, but it needs to be in full sun and on land that stays moist but is free draining. Its height makes it ideal for use in the middle to back of a herbaceous bed, or planted in bold drifts in a mixed border.

TIP
Bergamot spreads easily, but to keep it healthy, dig up the clump every few years, divide it and replant.

Sea holly (*Eryngium* spp.)

Flowering time:
■ Summer

When to plant:
■ Early to mid-spring

Height:
■ To 60cm (2ft)

Spread:
■ To 45cm (18in)

Hardiness:
■ Completely hardy

Sea holly is a wonderfully eye-catching plant, its heart-shaped, toothed, glossy foliage gives rise to stiff, lightly branching stems that are topped by purplish-blue flower heads surrounded by metallic-blue bracts.

Sea holly has the potential to benefit many insects, although it is bees that find it most irresistible. They often congregate in large numbers to seek out the nectar-rich, thistle-like flowers. Butterflies and beetles occasionally visit, too.

A native of the coast, sea holly is both drought- and wind-tolerant. Although it is unfussy about its soil type, it does need full sun and a free-draining site, making it ideal for a dry or exposed garden. It is a versatile plant, however, and is equally at home in formal borders.

TIP
This is an ideal plant for any Mediterranean garden. Its beautiful, purplish-blue colours contrast well with silvers, pinks and purples.

Mullein (*Verbascum* spp.)

Flowering time:
■ Mid-summer to early autumn
When to plant:
■ Spring
Height:
■ Up to 2m (6ft), according to the species and conditions
Spread:
■ To 60cm (2ft)
Hardiness:
■ Completely hardy

Mullein is a tall, majestic plant grown as a biennial or short-lived perennial. The plants form a dense, low rosette of often very hairy leaves, from which the flower stem ascends, topped by hundreds of small, pretty blooms. The flowers of different species vary in colour and while they are most commonly yellow, they can also be orange, red-brown, purple or white.

The flowers are very attractive to a range of insects including bees, which are frequent visitors, collecting the copious pollen for their larvae. Butterflies and smaller beetle species will also occasionally take nectar from the flowers.

For best results, plant mullein in full sun, ideally in well-drained soil, and although it will grow in almost any type of soil, it prefers chalky ground. This plant gives structure and height to herbaceous or mixed borders and can look great randomly spaced between grasses and other flowers in a dry border.

TIP
Mulleins can become very tall, so to get the best from them throughout their flowering season, it is a good idea to stake them.

Black-eyed Susan (*Rudbeckia fulgida*)

Flowering time:
- Late summer to mid- or late autumn

When to plant:
- Autumn or spring

Height:
- To 90cm (3ft)

Spread:
- 45cm (18in)

Hardiness:
- Completely hardy

Black-eyed Susans are a type of coneflower with large, golden, disc-shaped blooms, the colour of which is intensified by the almost black, velvety centres. The flowers open in huge abundance from early September, continuing in succession until early November.

The flowers are visited by bees attracted to the nectar. They are also very popular with late-flying butterflies, such as painted ladies and small tortoiseshells – in early to mid-autumn. As a late source of nectar they can be almost invaluable in helping insects reach peak condition prior to hibernation.

Although they will grow in almost any soil, they do need a sunny spot and are great for planting in bold drifts in borders. They make ideal companions for other late-summer performers, adding a much-needed boost to the autumn garden.

TIP
They look particularly impressive growing alongside plants such as Michaelmas daisies, dahlias, and ornamental grasses.

Michaelmas daisies (*Aster* spp.)

Flowering time:
■ Autumn
When to plant:
■ Spring
(preferably)
or autumn
Height:
■ To 1.2m (4ft)
Spread:
■ To 90cm (3ft)
Hardiness:
■ Completely
hardy

Michaelmas daisies are arguably the classic autumn perennial, providing a welcome boost of nectar in gardens as winter approaches. The tall stems are topped with masses of small, violet-blue flowers with yellow centres that seem to glow with colour, even on the dullest autumn day.

The nectar-rich flowers are a real favourite with butterflies, especially species like peacocks and tortoiseshells, when preparing to overwinter. The rich nectar helps to build up their body weight to aid them through the hibernation months, while the seeds that follow provide food for various birds, such as crossbills and finches.

A sunny spot is essential if Michaelmas daisies are to thrive, and they prefer soil that is slightly moist. The taller, old-fashioned types tend to lose their lower leaves and so are best placed towards the back of the border.

TIP
Many newer cultivars are available, including numerous dwarf forms, well suited to pots or window boxes.

Purpletop vervain (*Verbena bonariensis*)

Flowering time:
- Mid-summer until mid- to late autumn

When to plant:
- Spring

Height:
- To 2m (6ft)

Spread:
- 45cm (18in)

Hardiness:
- Generally quite hardy

Purpletop vervain is one of the best 'wildlife' plants available to gardeners. This short-lived perennial's clusters of nectar-rich, purple flowers are borne at the top of stiff, wiry stems. Clouds of butterflies, bees and moths are drawn to these flowers throughout the summer until the early frosts.

This is probably the best nectar plant for garden butterflies, because it flowers for a long period, continuing when many other nectar plants have finished. In addition to butterflies, bees and day- and night-flying moths also frequent the flowers.

A sunny site and a reasonably well-drained garden soil are all you need to grow purpletop vervain. Once established, it seeds freely around the garden.

TIP
Dot it among other plants in a border or arrange in solid drifts along the sunny side of a path or patio, so you can watch the visiting butterflies.

Purple coneflower (*Echinacea purpurea*)

Flowering time:
- Mid-summer to early autumn

When to plant:
- Spring (preferably) or autumn

Height:
- To 1.5m (5ft)

Spread:
- 45cm (18in)

Hardiness:
- Completely hardy

Purple coneflower is a beautiful, erect, daisy-flowered perennial that is both eye- catching and attracts numerous species of wildlife. The deep pink flower heads, borne singly in late summer, are actually made up of many small flowers that lack petals and are concentrated in the central, conical, brown-pink 'button' of the daisy head. The outer ring of petals serves only to attract flying insect visitors.

Purple coneflowers are very popular with bees and, more occasionally, butterflies and hoverflies. All of these visit the tiny nectar-rich flowers that make up the conical brown centre of the flower head.

Coneflowers need a rich, well-drained soil and although they grow best in full sun, they will tolerate partial shade. These versatile garden plants can be used in a variety of situations, being equally attractive planted in large, naturalistic drifts with ornamental grasses, or in more formal herbaceous or mixed borders.

TIP
Plants are quite long-lasting, but older ones can die for no apparent reason, so take cuttings occasionally as a precaution.

Eau naturelle

Garden ponds are relatively easy to construct, but they do need to be properly sited and designed in order for them to be useful as habitats. Choose a sunny spot that's sheltered from strong winds. Avoid overhanging trees as they cut out light and the fallen leaves pollute the water.

Form the outline of your pond using sweeping curves with no sharp bends, and aim to get a depth of at least 60cm (2ft), with shallower shelves and gently sloping sides for best effect. The slopes should drop away at roughly one-third of the distance across the top to ensure stability.

Promote a natural effect by varying the pond edge between areas of stones or cobbles and planted edges with lots of overhanging foliage. Use a range of plants in the water itself.

TIP

A patch of dense vegetation adjoining the pond will not only look good, but will also provide cover for animals as they approach or leave.

Waterside retreat

You will need:
- Plenty of flat pieces of rock
- Ready-mix mortar
- Plants to grow around and through the feature

A dry-stone wall or loose rock pile placed at the edge of a wildlife pond not only looks great, but also has the dual role of acting as a retaining wall for nearby planting. The niches between the stones provide shelter for many creatures, including reptiles and insects, as well as pond dwellers such as amphibians.

The wall base is set on to mortar just below the water level, so that it emerges from the pond itself. Place your dry-stone feature so that you will be looking across the water towards it – ideally with some surrounding vegetation so that the whole thing creates a reflection on the pool surface.

A dry-stone wall combines well with rocky shallows, which allow garden creatures to drink safely at the edge. A few larger stones can be placed and cemented in shallow water, and the spaces between loosely filled with smaller pebbles to create a series of little pools.

TIP
Alternatively, you can fill wire cages (gabions) with an assortment of stone shapes and these will remain stable.

Drawing in dragonflies

You will need:
- Pond, ideally with a surface area of at least 3.75 square metres (40 square feet)
- Shelter from winds, particularly those from the north and east
- Sunny location
- Variety of plants

All dragonflies are reliant on water; this is where they lay their eggs and is the habitat for the immature larval stage or nymph. They spend one to three years as nymphs then climb out of the water and up the stems of marginal plants as adults.

All dragonfly species need a stable pond environment, as well as good feeding and roosting sites, so you need to provide these if you want them to breed in your garden.

Plant a dragonfly pond with plenty of submerged vegetation to provide both a habitat and oxygen for the developing larvae. Also add a number of marginal plants in the shallower reaches to enable the larvae to climb out of the water and to provide perching, roosting and egg-laying sites for adults.

Suitable plants include: submerged ones such as *Callitriche stagnalis* (common water starwort), *Hottonia palustris* (water violet) and *Myriophyllum spicatum* (spiked water-milfoil); floating plants such as *Nymphaea* 'Pygmaea Helvola' (pigmy water lily), *Hydrocharis morsus ranae* (frogbit) and *Ranunculus aquatilis* (common water crowfoot); and marginals such as *Butomus umbellatus*, (flowering rush), *Iris pseudacorus* (yellow flag iris) and *Typha minima* (dwarf bulrush).

TIP
Warmth is essential, and the best breeding ponds are those that are sunny and sheltered from the wind.

Hop to it

You will need:
- Pond in a sunny part of the garden
- At least one gently sloping edge to the pond
- Vegetation in and around the pond
- Shelter, such as rock and log piles on land, near to the pond

Frogs are among the best-known wild visitors to garden ponds. They are frequently depicted in popular culture and are endlessly fascinating for children, and indeed many adults. These familiar creatures greatly enhance the natural balance in your garden, and their presence is a sure sign of a healthy, natural habitat.

Even a small pond can attract frogs, provided it is in a sunny part of the garden and has a gently sloping edge on at least one side. Plenty of vegetation, both in and around the pond, will provide shade and shelter for them while they are in the water, as well as when they come and go from the pond.

Let amphibians colonise naturally, as you run the risk of spreading disease if you move animals from another pond. If they don't arrive by themselves there could be many explanations. Still, the pond that you have built will still provide valuable shelter and water for a whole range of other creatures.

TIP
Avoid using pesticides in your garden and this will encourage lots of insects that will lure in frogs.

Give your pond the all-clear

You will need:
- Fresh barley straw – around 50g per square metre of pond surface
- Netting or string

During the summer months, algae can become a real problem in garden ponds, blocking pumps and filters and transforming crystal clear water into a dense, green, slimy mess. They can even pose a health hazard to humans, pets and wildlife.

Algae are difficult to control, mainly because herbicides can harm pond life and would kill the plants you want to keep, too. All is not lost, though, and adding barley straw to water rapidly kills off the algae without any damaging side-effects.

Simply tie balls of barley straw together or net them loosely, then float them on the pond, using around 50g of straw per square metre of water surface. As the straw rots, chemicals are released, preventing algal growth. The effect lasts for around six months, although they can take a couple of weeks to get going.

TIP
Start this off in early spring, before algae have had a chance to take hold.

Pool in a pot

You will need:

- Tin bath or other large container
- Waterproof sealant
- Bricks
- 2–3 medium planting baskets
- Small bag of aquatic compost
- Assortment of aquatic plants, including oxygenating plants
- Washed pea gravel

Patios and courtyard gardens may seem like the wrong place for a wildlife pond, but a raised pond can be easily and effectively incorporated into quite small spaces. If the proper balance between planting and the surroundings is achieved, even the smallest of barrels can become a mini-wildlife haven.

The type of container you use is not particularly important, and any large tin bath, wooden half-barrel, ornamental flower pot or similar water-tight container can be used. Remember that visiting wildlife may need help to get to the water, so it is a good idea to provide a 'ladder' of bricks or rocks inside and out.

Avoid large or quick-growing plants for the pond, opting instead for small plants such as pygmy water lilies and the dwarf bulrush. Ensure the pool isn't too isolated from the rest of the garden, and ideally place plenty pots of vegetation around it.

TIP
Try to incorporate a large rock into your pond, a little taller than the height of the container, to act as a 'basking island' for visiting animals.

Working with children and animals...

- Old bath or other suitably large container
- Mastic sealant
- Wedges to stop the container rocking
- Bricks, rocks or long thick branches for wildlife ladders
- Bricks to make shallow platforms for marginal plants
- Assortment of aquatic plants, including oxygenating plants

In any garden where a water feature is planned, child safety is a major consideration. Even if you think there is no risk that young children will visit, it's worth bearing in mind that most children who drown in a pond do so at someone else's house.

A raised pond is often the safest option, but you should always weigh up the risks. Be vigilant – make sure it is easily visible from all parts of the garden and always supervised when children are around it.

Having said this, children love water and the wildlife it attracts, and not to have some water in a garden is a real shame for all concerned. Ponds offer great learning potential for children, as they can see nature 'in the raw' from close proximity.

TIP

A secure grid of standard concrete-reinforcing mesh is ideal over the surface of a pond. It allows young children and ponds to co-exist safely, while allowing wildlife to come and go unhindered from the pond.

Island paradise

You will need:

- Pallet
- 4–6 large empty 5-litre plastic bottles, tops on
- Nylon string
- Untreated fence panel
- Small piece of rough turf
- Two or more synthetic ropes
- Two or more plant pots
- Small quantity of concrete

Ducks and other water fowl, while common across the country, only usually visit larger ponds. If you want them to nest there, you will need to give them an island. This offers not only a secure nest site, but also a place where they can roost overnight, safe from predators such as foxes.

The easiest way to do this is to add a floating island. This can be made from a pallet, preferably unpainted, under which you tie four to six large (5-litre) plastic bottles, with the tops on, to provide buoyancy.

Tie an untreated fence panel – a hazel hurdle is ideal – to the pallet and cover around two-thirds of this with some rough turf. Float your island into the pond.

TIP
Keep the island in open water by anchoring it using two or more synthetic ropes tied to the island and also to plant pots concreted into the pond.

Basket case

You will need:
- Aquatic basket
- Hessian sacking
- Small bag of aquatic compost
- Water plant
- Pea shingle or gravel
- Baby bath or trough

Marginal plants grow in shallow water at the edge of a pond, offering shade and cover, as well as looking great. Deep-water aquatics have roots and stems in the deeper reaches, but floating leaves and flowers. Both naturally root into soil, but in a pond they are best planted in specialist compost and aquatic baskets.

Cover the base of the basket with gravel, before adding the plants. Fill around the remaining gaps with compost to the height of the root ball, before dressing the surface with more gravel to help keep it in place. Thoroughly soak the basket in a large container of water for an hour to ensure that it will sink.

Carefully lower the basket into the pool, ensuring that it remains upright as it descends.

TIP
Water plants establish best if planted in early spring, quickly sending new shoots and flowers above the water surface.

Bubbling under

- Native oxygenating plants
- String, soft wire or a soft metal band
- A large stone

Plants that spend the whole year submerged are described as oxygenators, as they supply a steady infusion of oxygen into the water. This is needed by the multitude of aquatic creatures that breathe though gills. Oxygenators also serve as egg-laying sites, nurseries and hiding places for many aquatic animal species, and are vital to the health of a pond.

To plant them, simply take a few sections of stems and loosely tie them together. Attach a stone as an anchor, then place into the pond. The plants will grow readily and soon multiply, needing little attention except to be thinned out occasionally once established.

A few species of pond plant are entirely free floating. These include the familiar duckweed, but also some invasive alien species such as the water fern. Avoid planting any such invasive alien plants in your pond.

TIP
Oxygenators tend to be rather invasive unless closely managed, so are best avoided if you don't have time to keep them in check.

Water lily (*Nymphaea* 'Pygmaea Helvola')

Flowering time:
■ Mid- to late summer
When to plant:
■ Mid- to late spring
Height:
■ Floats in around 20cm (8in) of water
Spread:
■ 30–60cm (1–2ft)
Hardiness:
■ Hardy

While many water lilies are too big for a small garden pond, this pygmy type, with its exotic flowers, is ideal for even the tiniest pool. The dainty, cup-shaped, semi-double flowers are lemon-yellow with darker centres and are freely produced throughout the summer.

Water lilies enjoy a sunny position in still water and are a valuable addition to the pond, due to their ability to absorb toxins and keep the water 'sweet'. Plant the water lily in an aquatic basket and place it approximately 8–10cm (3–4in) below the surface of the water initially, before moving it down to 16-20cm (6–8in) once growth has begun.

Water lily flowers are visited by a range of insects, but are particularly favoured by beetles. The thick, floating leaf pads are used by basking frogs and dragonflies, and even foraging water birds. Water-bound pond life will also appreciate the shade they offer during the summer months.

TIP
Cover the compost in the aquatic basket with a 2.5cm (1in) layer of gravel before lowering into the water, to prevent the soil clouding the water.

Ragged robin (*Lychnis flos-cuculi*)

Flowering time:
- Late spring

When to plant:
- Autumn
or spring

Height:
- 75cm (30in)

Spread:
- 80cm (32in)

Hardiness:
- Completely
hardy

Ragged robin gains its name from the bright pink flowers with deeply divided petals that give it a 'ragged' look. These blooms, while delicate, are very showy and earn this plant a deserved place in the wildlife garden.

The nectar-rich flowers attract many species of insect, including hoverflies, honey bees, several species of long-tongued bee, and butterflies, from late spring onwards.

Growing naturally in water meadows, it is ideally suited to a sunny or slightly shaded spot, in damp grassland or a bog garden, where soil conditions, while not permanently waterlogged, do hold moisture all year round. It is a relatively short-lived plant, although the species seeds freely given the correct soil conditions.

TIP
The single-flowered white form, 'Alba', is an ideal choice, but avoid any double-flowered cultivars, as they produce much less nectar.

Marsh marigold *(Caltha palustris)*

Flowering time:
- Early spring

When to plant:
- Sow seed in autumn, or plant in early spring or autumn

Height:
- 60cm (2ft)

Spread:
- 30–60cm (1–2ft)

Hardiness:
- Completely hardy

The beautiful, single, bright golden-yellow flowers of the marsh marigold are a truly welcome sight in early spring, when, as the name suggests, they appear in the damp margins of the pond. The plant's compact habit and lush dark green foliage, which acts as an effective foil for the bright flowers, make it deservedly popular with gardeners.

The marsh marigold is best grown in permanently moist soil or just submerged on shelving around a pond edge, in full sun or light shade. It combines well with other waterside plants, but can also be planted in drifts next to larger ponds and along stream sides.

Being one of the first spring flowers, marsh marigolds are an early source of nectar for bees and butterflies emerging from hibernation. The dense foliage offers shelter for small insects such as beetles and amphibians.

TIP

Avoid using double-flowered cultivars such as 'Flore Pleno', as they offer little nectar.

Hemp agrimony (*Eupatorium cannabinum*)

Flowering time:
- Late summer

When to plant:
- Plant or sow seed in spring

Height:
- 2m (6ft)

Spread:
- 60cm (2ft) or more

Hardiness:
- Completely hardy

Hemp agrimony is a vigorous, tall-growing, herbaceous perennial. It sports large, fluffy, pale dusty-pink or whitish-pink flower heads, made up of many tiny starry flowers, from summer to early autumn.

It is a truly superb plant for the wildlife pond – the flowers are literally heaving with insects in mid- to late summer, particularly butterflies such as small tortoiseshells, red admirals and peacocks. Bees are also frequent visitors, searching for both pollen and nectar.

Due to its size, it may not be well suited for use around small ponds. However, this is a versatile plant, being most at home in a bog garden, ideally in partial shade, as prolonged periods of strong sunlight cause wilting.

TIP
The plants are either male or female, so several should be grown to ensure both nectar and pollen are produced.

Purple loosestrife (*Lythrum salicaria*)

Flowering time:
- Mid-summer to early autumn

When to plant:
- Plant in the autumn or sow seed in spring

Height:
- Up to 90cm (3ft)

Spread:
- 60cm (2ft) or more

Hardiness:
- Completely hardy

Few, if any, garden plants are the equal of purple loosestrife when planted around a pond. The tall, brightly coloured blooms are spectacular when they appear over several weeks in mid-summer to early autumn. A mature plant can have as many as 30 flowering stems, meaning that even a single specimen can be a dramatic addition to the garden.

The flowers are popular with bees and butterflies, and the leaves are eaten by the caterpillars of the emperor and small elephant hawk moths.

Purple loosestrife is an ideal choice for pond margins or bog gardens, as the roots thrive in soil that is moist or wet. It is equally well suited to the dappled shade of a woodland garden, provided the soil is moist and rich in organic matter.

TIP
Don't cut down the stems in late autumn, as beneficial insects will hibernate in the dead foliage over winter.

Dwarf bulrush (*Typha minima*)

Flowering time:
- Summer

When to plant:
- Sow seed, divide or plant in spring

Height:
- 45–60cm (18–24in)

Spread:
- Unlimited (if allowed)

Hardiness:
- Completely hardy

Dwarf bulrush is grown for its decorative, poker-like, cylindrical seed heads that form in late summer. The male flowers appear in summer as small tufts above the familiar 'bulrush' head, which is the female flower spike.

The fluffy seed heads are often used by birds for nesting material, while dragonfly nymphs use the emerging stems to climb out of the water. The intricate root system gathers pond silt and debris and provides a breeding ground for pond invertebrates as well as a site for over-wintering amphibians.

Plant dwarf bulrushes in the shallows of pond margins, either in soil or baskets, in sun or part shade. In larger pools, particularly those without a synthetic liner, their intricate root system can be used to stabilise the banks.

TIP
This is a great plant, but beware of the roots, as these bear needle-like tips that can easily pierce flexible liners.

Index

Picture credits

BBC Books and *Gardeners' World Magazine* would like to thank the following for providing photographs. While every effort has been made to trace and acknowledge all photographers, we should like to apologise should there be any errors or omissions.

BBC Books p205, p209; Torie Chugg p159, p177; Eric Crichton p55; Sarah Cuttle p9, p11, p17, p23, p27, p33, p37, p59, p81, p83, p85, p99, p101, p111, p113, p123, p125, p129, p137, p145; Paul Debois p13, p15, p25, p29, p87, p91, p105, p131, p133, p141, p153, p189, p191; Dig Pictures/Freia Turland p161; Stephen Hamilton p173; Jason Ingram p31, p61, p63, p89, p103, p119, p139, p165, p171, p175, p179, p181, p187, p193, p195, p197, p199, p201, p207; Lynn Keddie p53, p135, p163, p169; Stephen Marwood p51; David Murray p95, p157, p183; Adrian Myers p127; Adam Pasco p35; Tim Sandall p19, p21, p39, p41, p45, p49, p67, p71, p73, p75, p77, p79, p93, p97, p107, p109, p117, p121, p149, p185, p203; William Shaw p65, p147, p151, p155; John Trenholm p57, p69, p167; Jo Whitworth p43, p115; Mark Winwood p47

We would also like to thank all our contributors who helped originate these ideas for *Gardeners' World Magazine*, including Lisa Buckland, Jayne Keeley, Mick Lavelle, Helen Riches.